Bangladesh
Travel Guide 2024

Discover Bangladesh : Your Comprehensive
guide to A Journey Through the Soul of the
Sundarbans

By

Anna V. Jones

Table of content

Sample itineraries
Packing Checklist

Introduction

Settled between the transcending pinnacles of the Himalayas toward the north and the purplish blue influxes of the Strait of Bengal toward the south, Bangladesh is a place that is known for energetic scenes, rich history, and pleasant individuals. Welcome to "Finding Bangladesh," your visa to an uncommon experience through this frequently neglected pearl of South Asia.

As you turn the pages of this movement guide, you'll leave on a spellbinding odyssey that will take you from clamouring metropolitan roads to quiet wide open vistas, from old archeological wonders to contemporary social celebrations. Bangladesh is a country that winds around an embroidery of variety, and we're here to direct you through each string.

In these pages, you will reveal the secret fortunes of Cox's Bazar, the world's longest regular oceanside, and the mysterious Sundarbans, home to the tricky Imperial Bengal Tiger. You'll walk around the memorable paths of Old Dhaka, where time appears to stop, and dive into the quiet excellence of the Sylhet tea gardens.

However, this book isn't just about places; it's about individuals. You'll meet local people whose accounts and accommodation will make a permanent imprint on your excursion. From the anglers on the banks of the Padma Stream to the craftsmans creating many-sided Nakshi Kantha, you'll encounter the spirit of Bangladesh through their eyes.

Whether you're a valiant pioneer looking for experience, a set of experiences devoted to following the strides of realms, or a food sweetheart anxious to enjoy the delightful kinds of Bangladeshi cooking, "Finding Bangladesh" is your manual for an extraordinary endeavour.

Thus, open your heart and your psyche to the charm of this enthralling nation, where at various times meet in an agreeable mix. Go along with us as we leave on a captivating investigation of Bangladesh, a land ready to be found.

Allow your excursion to start.

Chapter 1: Welcome to Bangladesh

Geography and Location

Bangladesh is a thickly populated, low-lying, mostly riverine country situated in South Asia with a shore of 720 km (447 mi) on the northern littoral of the Strait of Bengal. The delta plain of the Ganges (Padma), Brahmaputra (Jamuna), and Meghna Streams and their feeders possess 79% of the country. Four elevated blocks (remembering the Madhupur and Barind Lots for the middle and northwest) possess 9% and steep slope ranges up to roughly 1,000 metres (3,300 ft) high involve 12% in the southeast (the Chittagong Slope Plots) and in the upper east.

Bangladesh is on the west, north, and east by a 4,095 kilometres (2,545 mi) land wilderness with India and, in the southeast, by a short land and water boondocks (193 kilometres (120 mi)) with Myanmar. On the south is an exceptionally unpredictable deltaic shore of around 580 kilometres (360 mi), fissured by numerous waterways and streams streaming into the Narrows of Bengal. The regional waters of Bangladesh expand 12 nautical miles (22 km), and the selective financial zone of the nation is 200 nautical miles (370 km).

The topography of Bangladesh is still up in the air by the Ganges, Brahmaputra, and Meghna Waterways, which structure the world's biggest stream delta. The delta is a low-lying region that is inclined to flooding during the rainstorm season. The nation likewise has various streams and channels, which are utilised for transportation and water systems.

The environment of Bangladesh is tropical, with sweltering summers and gentle winters. The storm season endures from June to October, and during this time the nation gets heavy precipitation. Bangladesh is additionally helpless against typhoons and other catastrophic events.

The geology and area of Bangladesh essentially affect its economy and society. The prolific delta land is great for horticulture, and the nation is a significant maker of rice, jute, and different yields. The waterways and trenches are likewise significant for transportation and exchange. Nonetheless, the country's weakness to catastrophic events is a significant test, and flooding and typhoons can cause far reaching harm and death toll.

Regardless of its difficulties, Bangladesh is a wonderful and diverse country with a rich culture and legacy. Individuals of Bangladesh are tough and clever, and they have gained huge headway as of late in working on their way of life.

Brief History and Culture

Bangladesh has a long and richterm history, going back more than 4,000 years. The locale has been controlled by a progression of Hindu, Buddhist, and Muslim realms throughout the long . Islam turned into the predominant religion in the thirteenth 100 years, and today Bangladesh is a Muslim-greater part country.

In 1947, the English Indian Domain was apportioned into two free nations: India and Pakistan. East Bengal, which is presently Bangladesh, turned out to be essential for Pakistan. Be that as it may, East Bengal was geologically isolated from the remainder of Pakistan by more than 1,000 miles of Indian region. This made it challenging for the Pakistani government to successfully oversee East Bengal.

In 1971, East Bengal declared its freedom from Pakistan. This prompted a nine-month battle between the two nations, which brought about the deaths of millions of individuals. Bangladesh at long last acquired its freedom on December 16, 1971.

Bangladeshi culture

Bangladeshi culture is a rich and various mix of impacts from Hinduism, Buddhism, and Islam. The nation is likewise home to various ethnic minorities, each with its own one of a kind culture and customs.

Music and dance

Music and dance assume a significant part in Bangladeshi culture. There are various kinds of Bangladeshi music, including old style, society, and current. Bangladeshi dance is likewise extremely different, and incorporates various styles like Kathak, Bharatnatyam, and Manipuri.

Writing

Bangladesh has a rich scholarly practice, tracing all the way back to the thirteenth 100 years. Probably the most well known Bangladeshi journalists incorporate Rabindranath Tagore, Kazi Nazrul Islam, and Humayun Ahmed.

Workmanship and design

Bangladeshi workmanship and design are likewise affected by the country's different strict and social legacy. Probably the most renowned Bangladeshi landmarks incorporate the Somapura Mahavihara, a Buddhist religious community complex tracing all the way back to the eighth 100 years, and the Ahsan Manzil, a previous royal residence of the Nawab of Dhaka.

Food

Bangladeshi food is known for its rich flavours and flavours. The absolute most well known Bangladeshi dishes incorporate rice, fish, meat, vegetables, and lentils. Bangladeshi individuals likewise partake in various sweet dishes, for example, rasgulla and jalebi.

Celebrations

Bangladesh praises various celebrations consistently. The absolute most well known celebrations incorporate Eid al-Fitr, Eid al-Adha, Durga Puja, and Bijoy Dibos.

Bangladesh is a country with a rich and different culture. The nation's kin are glad for their legacy, and they are generally glad to impart it to guests.

Visa and Travel Essentials

Visa

Residents of most nations require a visa to enter Bangladesh. Visas can be gotten ahead of time from a Bangladeshi international safe haven or department, or upon landing in specific ports of section.

Visa on appearance

The accompanying identities are qualified for a visa on appearance in Bangladesh:

All SAARC nations aside from Afghanistan

China

Hong Kong

Indonesia

Japan

Macau

Malaysia
Maldives
Mauritius
Mongolia
Montenegro
Nepal
Norway
Oman
Qatar
Russia
Serbia
Singapore
South Korea
Sri Lanka
Thailand
Turkey
Joined Middle Easterner Emirates
Joined Realm
US

To get a visa on appearance, you should give a substantial identification no less than a half year remaining legitimacy, a return or forward ticket, and verification of adequate assets to help your visit. You will likewise have to finish a visa application structure and pay a visa expense.

Travel basics

Here are a few fundamental things to pack for your outing to Bangladesh:

Visa
Visa (whenever required)pll3
Return or ahead ticket
Confirmation of adequate assets
Travel protection
Meds (if necessary)
Bug repellent
Sunscreen
Cap
Scarf or wrap
Agreeable shoes
Light, baggy dress
Toiletries
Camera
Connector plug (if necessary)
Other travel tips
Bangladesh is a Muslim-greater part country, so it is critical to consciously dress. Ladies ought to cover their shoulders and knees, and men ought to try not to wear shorts out in the open spots.

The authority language of Bangladesh is Bengali, however English is broadly spoken in metropolitan regions.

The money of Bangladesh is the taka (BDT). You can trade money at banks, lodgings, and cash trade departments.

Mastercards are acknowledged at significant lodgings and cafés, yet it is consistently smart to have some money close by.

The environment of Bangladesh is hot and damp, so it is critical to remain hydrated and wear sunscreen. Bangladesh is a moderately protected country to go in, however it is generally really smart to know about your environmental factors and play it safe against negligible burglary.

Have an incredible excursion to Bangladesh!

Chapter 2. Planning Your Trip to Bangladesh

Bangladesh is a South Asian nation known for its lavish green scenes, different culture, and cordial individuals. It is a well known traveller location for its normal magnificence, verifiable destinations, and strict importance.

When to go

The best chance to visit Bangladesh is during the dry season, which runs from October to Spring. During this time, the weather conditions are gentle and radiant, and there is less precipitation. The stormy season endures from April to September, and can be very hot and moist.

Arriving

Hazrat Shahjalal Global Air terminal in Dhaka is the vitally worldwide air terminal in Bangladesh. There are non-stop trips to Dhaka from many significant urban communities all over the planet, including London, New York, Delhi, and Dubai.

Visa necessities

Most guests to Bangladesh require a visa. Visas can be gotten on the web or at a Bangladeshi government office or department.

What should be done

Bangladesh brings something to the table for everybody, from its clamouring urban areas to its tranquil open country. Here are the absolute most well known vacation destinations in Bangladesh:

Dhaka: The capital city of Bangladesh, Dhaka is an energetic and clamouring city. It is home to various authentic and social attractions, including the Lalbagh Stronghold, the Public Historical centre, and the Dhakeshwari Public Sanctuary.

Cox's Bazar: Cox's Bazar is the longest ocean side on the planet, and is a famous objective for swimming, sunbathing, and water sports.

Sylhet: Sylhet is a delightful city in northeastern Bangladesh known for its tea manors, lavish green woods, and cascades.

Chittagong: Chittagong is the second biggest city in Bangladesh and is a significant port city. It is home to various verifiable and social attractions, including the Pahartali Slope, the Chittagong Zoo, and the Chittagong War Burial ground.

Bandarban: Bandarban is a slope region in southeastern Bangladesh known for its dazzling landscape, cascades, and ancestral culture.

Sreemangal: Sreemangal is a town in Sylhet Division known for its tea manors, rich green woodlands, and cascades.

Bagerhat: Bagerhat is an UNESCO World Legacy Site known for its very much saved mosques, burial places, and other verifiable landmarks.

Sundarbans: The Sundarbans is the world's biggest mangrove woodland and is home to an assortment of natural life, including the Bengal tiger.

Getting around

The most ideal way to get around Bangladesh is by transport or train. Transports are the most reasonable choice, yet can be packed and slow. Trains are more agreeable and quicker, yet can be more costly. There are likewise various homegrown carriers that work trips between significant urban communities.

Food and drink

Bangladeshi cooking is a combination of Indian and Mughal impacts. It is known for its utilisation of flavours and its range of dishes. Probably the most famous Bangladeshi dishes incorporate biryani, kebabs, and naan bread.

Where to remain

There is an extensive variety of convenience choices accessible in Bangladesh, from financial plan lodgings to lavish inns. The best put to remain will rely upon your financial plan and inclinations.

Tips for explorers

The following are a couple of tips for explorers to Bangladesh:

Be ready for the intensity and mugginess, particularly on the off chance that you are visiting throughout the mid year months.

Dress unobtrusively, particularly while visiting strict locales.

Know about your environmental elements and play it safe to keep away from pickpocketing and different tricks.

Gain proficiency with a couple of fundamental Bengali expressions, for example, "hi," "thank you," and farewell.

Be patient and understanding. Things may not generally work out as expected in Bangladesh, yet that is essential for the experience.

With its shocking view, rich culture, and well disposed individuals, Bangladesh is a country that brings something to the table for everybody.

Best Time to Visit

The best chance to visit Bangladesh is throughout the colder time of year, from November to February. During this time, the weather conditions are wonderful, with normal temperatures going from 12 to 30 degrees Celsius. The skies are clear and bright, and there is less precipitation. This makes it an extraordinary opportunity to investigate the country's numerous normal attractions, for example, the Sundarbans mangrove woods, the Chittagong Slope Parcels, and the Imperial Bengal Public Park.

Walk and April are additionally great times to visit Bangladesh, as the weather conditions are still generally gentle and there are less travellers. Notwithstanding, it is vital to take note that the temperature can begin to rise in April, so it is essential to be ready for a hotter climate.

May to October is the storm season in Bangladesh, and weighty precipitation can make it hard to travel and partake in the outside. Nonetheless, the rainstorm season likewise draws out the country's lavish vegetation and plentiful natural life. On the off chance that you wouldn't fret the downpour, the storm season can be an extraordinary opportunity to visit Bangladesh and experience its remarkable culture and customs.

Here is a more point by point breakdown of the various seasons in Bangladesh:

Summer (Walk May): Hot and muggy, with temperatures frequently arriving at north of 40 degrees Celsius.

Storm (June-October): Weighty precipitation, particularly in the southeastern piece of the country.

Winter (November-February): Lovely climate, with normal temperatures going from 12 to 30 degrees Celsius.

Things to remember while arranging your excursion:

In the event that you are wanting to visit during the storm season, make certain to pack light, waterproof dress and downpour gear.

Bangladesh is a Muslim nation, so it is essential to differentially dress. This implies covering your shoulders and knees.

The authority language of Bangladesh is Bengali, yet English is broadly spoken in significant vacationer regions.

Bangladesh is a somewhat reasonable country to visit, however it is critical to spending plans for transportation, convenience, and food.

Travel Budgeting

Bangladesh is a moderately cheap country to go in, with a day to day spending plan of around $25-30 every day being adequate for most financial plan voyagers. This incorporates convenience, food, transportation, and exercises. Notwithstanding, to go in more solace or extravagance, the expense can be higher.

Here is a breakdown of a portion of the fundamental travel costs in Bangladesh:

Convenience

Spending plan guesthouse or lodging: $5-10 every evening

Mid-range inn: $20-30 every evening

Upscale hotel: $65+ each evening

Food

Nearby café feast: $3-5

Road food: $1-2

Transportation

Neighbourhood transport or cart ride: $1-2

Entire day taxi rental: $30-50

Exercises

Extra charges to traveller destinations: $5-10

Directed visits: $15-20

Here are a ways to get a good deal on your excursion to Bangladesh:

Go during the slow time of year (May-June and September-October). Costs for convenience and exercises are ordinarily lower during this time.

Remain in guesthouses or lodgings. These spending plan cordial facilities are spotless and agreeable, and they offer an extraordinary method for meeting different explorers.

Eat at neighbourhood cafés and road food slows down. The food in Bangladesh is delightful and reasonable, and it's an extraordinary method for encountering the nearby culture.

Take public transportation. Transports and trains are the least expensive method for getting around Bangladesh. In the event that you're going on a careful spending plan, try not to take taxis except if you need to.

Can anticipate labour and products. Bartering is normal in Bangladesh, and it's an extraordinary cash saving tip for everything from gifts to transportation.

Here is an example financial plan for a 7-roadtrip to Bangladesh:

Accommodation: $10-15 every evening

Food: $10-15 every day

Transportation: $5-10 every day

Exercises: $5-10 every day

All out: $30-40 every day

This spending plan is only a beginning stage, and you might have to change it relying upon your movement style and inclinations. For instance, to remain in more pleasant lodgings or eat at additional costly cafés, you'll have to spend more cash. On the other hand, on the off chance that you're willing to remain in guesthouses, eat road food, and take public transportation, you can set aside a ton of cash.

Itinerary Planning

Show up in Dhaka, the capital of Bangladesh. Look into your inn and leave your baggage. Go for a stroll around the downtown area and visit a portion of the fundamental attractions, for example, the Public Gallery, the Lalbagh Post, and the Dhakeshwari Sanctuary. At night, partake in a customary

Bangladeshi dinner at one of the numerous cafés in the city.

Require a roadtrip to the Sundarbans, the world's biggest mangrove woods. This UNESCO World Legacy Site is home to an assortment of untamed life, including the Bengal tiger. Take a boat visit through the woods and look out for these grand animals.

Fly to Chittagong, the second-biggest city in Bangladesh. Visit the Chittagong War Graveyard, the Ethnological Historical centre, and the Zia Dedication Exhibition hall. At night, go for a stroll along the Karnaphuli Stream and partake in the dusk.

Take a transport to Cox's Bazar, home to the world's longest solid oceanside. Go through the day loosening up around the ocean, swimming, and sunbathing. At night, partake in a fish supper at one of the numerous eateries along the ocean side.

Go on a boat outing to St. Martin's Island, a little island off the bank of Cox's Bazar. The island is known for its white sand sea shores, completely clear waters, and coral reefs. Go through the day swimming, swimming, and

Fly back to Dhaka. Visit the Ahsan Manzil, the Pink Royal residence, and the Curzon Lobby. At night, partake in a goodbye supper at one of the numerous eateries in the city.

Leave from Dhaka.

This is only a recommended schedule, and you can tweak it to accommodate your inclinations and spending plan. For instance, in the event that you are keen on climbing, you could put in a couple of days in the Chittagong Slope Plots. Or on the other hand, on the off chance that you are keen on culture, you could visit the Somapura Mahavihara, a Buddhist cloister in Paharpur.

Here are an extra ways to design your outing to Bangladesh:

The best opportunity to visit Bangladesh is throughout the cold weather months (November to February), when the weather conditions are gentle.

Bangladesh is a Muslim-greater part country, so it is essential to dress. Ladies ought to cover their shoulders and knees, and men ought to try not to wear shorts.

Bangladesh is a generally modest country to visit. You can hope to spend around $50-$100 each day on convenience, food, and exercises.

Make certain to get a visa before you travel to Bangladesh. You can apply for a visa at the Bangladeshi government office or department in your nation of origin.

Chapter 3. Exploring Top Destinations in Bangladesh

Bangladesh is a different country with a rich history and culture. It is home to dazzling regular magnificence, from the world's biggest mangrove timberland to the longest ocean side on the planet. Bangladesh is likewise an incredible spot to encounter real Bengali culture, with its delightful food, energetic music, and cordial individuals.

Here are a portion of the top objections to investigate in Bangladesh:

Cox's Bazar: Cox's Bazar is home to the world's longest regular oceanside, extending for 125 kilometres (78 miles). The ocean side is known for its white sand, clear water, and delicate waves. Cox's Bazar is a famous traveller objective for the two local people and outsiders, and it offers different exercises for guests, including swimming, sunbathing, surfing, and fishing.

Cox's Bazar Ocean side, Bangladesh

Sundarbans Public Park: The Sundarbans Public Park is the world's biggest mangrove backwoods, and it is home to an assortment of untamed life, including the Bengal tiger. The recreation area is an UNESCO World Legacy Site, and it is a famous objective for nature darlings and untamed life fans. Guests can go on boat voyages through the recreation area, and they might have the option to see tigers, crocodiles, dolphins, and different creatures.

Sundarbans Public Park, Bangladesh

Sreemangal: Sreemangal is a town in the Sylhet locale of Bangladesh that is known for its tea gardens. The town is encircled by rich green slopes and valleys, and it is a famous objective for nature darlings and tea lovers. Guests can go on voyages through the tea nurseries, and they can likewise attempt various sorts of tea at the nearby teahouses.

Bangladesh

Rangamati: Rangamati is a slope region in Bangladesh that is known for its normal magnificence and its native culture. The area is home to Kaptai Lake, which is quite possibly the biggest lake in Bangladesh. Guests can go on boat voyages through the lake, and they can likewise visit the native towns to find out about their way of life and lifestyle.

Kaptai Lake, Rangamati, Bangladesh

Bandarban: Bandarban is another slope area in Bangladesh that is known for its regular excellence and its native culture. The region is home to the Sajek Valley, which is one of the most famous vacationer locations in Bangladesh. Guests can go on journeys in the valley, and they can likewise visit the native towns to find out about their way of life and lifestyle.

Sajek Valley, Bandarban, Bangladesh
Notwithstanding these top objections, there are numerous other fascinating spots to visit in Bangladesh, like the capital city of Dhaka, the noteworthy city of Sonargaon, and the antiquated city of Mahasthangarh. Bangladesh is likewise home to various strict locales, like the Baitul Mukarram Public Mosque and the Shaheed Minar.

Dhaka, the Capital City

Dhaka is the capital and biggest city of Bangladesh. It is the 10th biggest and seventh-most thickly populated city on the planet. Dhaka is a megacity, and has a populace of 10.2 million occupants starting around 2022, and a populace of over 22.4 million inhabitants in More noteworthy Dhaka. Being the most thickly populated developed metropolitan region in the world is generally thought of. Dhaka is the most significant social, monetary, and logical centre of Eastern South Asia, as well as a significant Muslim-greater part city.

Dhaka is situated in the geographic focus of the country. It is in the extraordinary deltaic locale of the Ganges and Brahmaputra waterways. The city is arranged on the banks of the Buriganga Stream, a feeder of the Dhaleswari Waterway.

Dhaka has a long and rich history, tracing all the way back to the seventh 100 years. The city was first referenced in Quite a while in the seventh century Promotion. Dhaka turned into the capital of the Mughal territory of Bengal in the seventeenth hundred years, and it stayed the capital of Bengal until the parcel of India in 1947. After the segment, Dhaka turned into the capital of East Pakistan. In 1971, East Pakistan acquired freedom from Pakistan and turned into the new country of Bangladesh. Dhaka was assigned as the capital of Bangladesh.

Dhaka is a significant community for industry, trade, and instruction. The city is home to various huge companies, as well as a few colleges and schools. Dhaka is likewise a significant transportation centre point, with a global air terminal and a port.

Dhaka is a lively and cosmopolitan city. It is home to individuals from all over Bangladesh, as well as from numerous different nations. The city is known for its rich culture, tasty food, and agreeable individuals.

Here are a portion of the famous vacation destinations in Dhaka:

Public Parliament House: This notorious structure was planned by American planner Louis Khan. It is the seat of the Parliament of Bangladesh.

Ahsan Manzil: This previous castle was the home of the Nawab of Dhaka. Presently a historical centre houses an assortment of curios from the Mughal period.

Lalbagh Stronghold: This incomplete post was worked by Mughal ruler Aurangzeb in the seventeenth hundred years. It is presently a famous vacation spot.

Star Mosque: This mosque is popular for its star-moulded rooftop. It is quite possibly the most lovely mosque in Dhaka.

Dhakeshwari Sanctuary: This Hindu sanctuary is perhaps the main Hindu sanctuary in Bangladesh. It is committed to the goddess Durga.

On the off chance that you are arranging an outing to Bangladesh, make certain to add Dhaka to your schedule. A city brings something to the table for everybody.

Cox's Bazar and Beaches

Cox's Bazar is a city, fishing port, the travel industry focus, and locale central command in southeastern Bangladesh. The famous Cox's Bazar Ocean side, one of the most well known vacation destinations in Bangladesh, is the longest continuous ocean side on the planet. It is found 150 km (93 mi) south of the city of Chittagong.

Cox's Bazar Ocean side in Bangladesh

The ocean side in Cox's Bazar has a delicate slant and with a solid length of 155 km (96 mi) it is frequently called the "longest normal whole ocean side" on the planet. Cox's Bazar lies on a seaside plain in the southeastern corner of Bangladesh. From a higher place, the plain seems to swell out into the Sound of Bengal.

Cox's Bazar is a well known objective for both homegrown and global travellers. The ocean side is known for its white sand, clear blue water, and delicate waves. It is an incredible spot to swim, sunbathe, and unwind. There are likewise numerous exercises accessible for travellers, for example, boat visits, fishing, and parasailing.

Different sea shores in Cox's Bazar

Notwithstanding the principal Cox's Bazar Ocean side, there are numerous different sea shores nearby, each with its own remarkable appeal. Probably the most well known sea shores include:

Laboni Ocean side: This ocean side is situated around 6 km from Cox's Bazar town and is known for its lovely landscape and clean sand. It is a well known spot for swimming, sunbathing, and picnicking.

Laboni Ocean side in Bangladesh

Inani Ocean side: This ocean side is situated around 10 km from Cox's Bazar town and is known for its separated environment and completely clear water. It is an incredible spot to unwind and get away from the groups.

Inani Ocean side in Bangladesh

Himchari Oceanside: This ocean side is situated around 20 km from Cox's Bazar town and is known for its sensational precipices and cascades. It is a well known spot for travelling and touring.

Humchari Ocean side in Bangladesh

Teknaf Ocean side: This ocean side is situated at the southernmost tip of Bangladesh and is known for its distance and unblemished excellence. It is an extraordinary spot to take a dip, sunbathe, or just partake in harmony and calm.

Teknaf Ocean side in Bangladesh

What should be done in Cox's Bazar

As well as visiting the sea shores, there are numerous different activities in Cox's Bazar. The following are a couple of ideas:

Visit the Himchari Cascade: This cascade is situated around 15 km from Cox's Bazar town and is a famous spot for swimming and picnicking.

Himchari Cascade in Bangladesh

Go on a boat outing to Sonadia Island: This island is situated around 10 km from Cox's Bazar and is known for its delightful sea shores, mangrove timberlands, and coral reefs.

Sonadia Island in Bangladesh

Visit the Buddhist sanctuaries in Ramu: This town is situated around 30 km from Cox's Bazar and is home to various Buddhist sanctuaries, including the Kaptai Buddhist Sanctuary and the Sangu Valley Buddhist Sanctuary.

Kaptai Buddhist Sanctuary in Bangladesh

Visit the Kutupalong Outcast Camp: This camp is situated around 30 km from Cox's Bazar and is home to more than 1,000,000 Rohingya displaced people. It is the biggest exile camp on the planet.

Instructions to get to Cox's Bazar.

Cox's Bazar is associated with different pieces of Bangladesh by street, rail, and air. The closest air terminal is Cox's Bazar Air terminal, which is situated around 10 km from the town community. There are additionally normal train and transport administrations from Dhaka and Chittagong.

When to visit Cox's Bazar

The best chance to visit Cox's Bazar is throughout the cold weather months (October to Spring), when the weather conditions are gentle and bright. Be that as it may, the town is famous all year, so it is vital to book your convenience and exercises ahead of time, particularly assuming you are going during top season.

Ways to visit Cox's Bazar

Dress moderately: Bangladesh is a Muslim-larger part country, so it is vital to dress moderately, particularly while visiting strict locales.

Be ready for swarms: Cox's Bazar is a well known traveller objective, so it is essential to be ready for swarms, particularly during top season.

Sundarbans Mangrove Forest

The Sundarbans Mangrove Backwoods in Bangladesh is the biggest bordering mangrove woodland on the planet, covering an area of north of 10,000 square kilometres. It is situated in the delta of the Ganges, Brahmaputra, and Meghna waterways, and is divided among Bangladesh and India. The Sundarbans is an UNESCO World Legacy Site and is known for its rich biodiversity, including north of 450 types of natural life, including the Imperial Bengal tiger.

Sundarbans Mangrove Woods in Bangladesh
The Sundarbans mangrove woods is a special and significant environment. Mangrove trees are adjusted to living in saltwater, and their underlying foundations help to balance out the shoreline and safeguard against disintegration. Mangrove woods likewise give environment to a wide assortment of fish, birds, and other natural life.

The Sundarbans is home to various compromised and endangered species, including the Regal Bengal tiger, the estuarine crocodile, and the Indian python. The tiger is the most notable creature of the

Sundarbans, and the woods is home to the biggest populace of tigers on the planet.

The Sundarbans is additionally a significant monetary asset for Bangladesh. The woodland gives livelihoods to a huge number of individuals through fishing, ranger service, and the travel industry.

Notwithstanding, the Sundarbans is confronting various difficulties, including environmental change, ocean level ascent, and deforestation. Environmental change is causing more incessant and extreme tempests, which can harm the mangrove woodlands and uproot natural life. Ocean level ascent is likewise immersing mangrove timberlands and making them more defenceless against disintegration. Deforestation is a significant issue in the Sundarbans, as individuals clear mangrove woods for farming, hydroponics, and other improvement projects.

Regardless of the difficulties it faces, the Sundarbans remains an imperative environment for Bangladesh and the world. Safeguarding the Sundarbans and its biodiversity for people in the future is significant.

Here are a portion of the things that should be possible to safeguard the Sundarbans:

Decrease ozone harming substance outflows to alleviate environmental change and ocean level ascent.

Plant and reestablish mangrove woods.

Foster economic administration rehearses for the Sundarbans that safeguard its biodiversity and give livelihoods to nearby individuals.

Bring issues to light of the significance of the Sundarbans and the need to safeguard it.

Chittagong Hill Tracts

The Chittagong Slope Plots (CHT), frequently abbreviated to just the Slope Lots and truncated to CHT, are a gathering of locales inside the Chittagong Division in southeastern Bangladesh, lining India and Myanmar. Covering 13,295 square kilometres (5,133 sq mi), they framed a solitary region until 1984, when they were separated into three locales: Khagrachari Locale, Rangamati Slope Region, and Bandarban Area.

Geologically, the Slope Parcels are the main broadly bumpy region in Bangladesh. They are portrayed by moving slopes, lavish woodlands, and various waterways and streams. The most noteworthy point in the locale is Mowdok Mual, which ascends to a height of 1,052 metres (3,451 ft).

The Slope Plots are home to a different scope of ethnic gatherings, including the Chakma, Marma, Tripura, and Tanchangya. These native people groups have their own interesting societies, dialects, and religions. Most of the populace in the

Slope Lots is Buddhist, yet there are additionally critical Christian and Muslim minorities.

The Slope Plots are a locale of extraordinary regular excellence and biodiversity. They are home to an assortment of untamed life, including elephants, tigers, panthers, and monkeys. The locale is likewise home to various safeguarded regions, including the Sajek Valley Natural life Asylum, the Sangu Untamed life Safe-haven, and the Keokradong Public Park.

The Slope Parcels have a long and complex history. They have been possessed for millennia, and have been controlled by a wide range of realms and realms throughout the long term. In the twentieth 100 years, the Slope Parcels were a significant site of contention during the Bangladesh Freedom War.

Since the marking of the Chittagong Slope Plots International agreement in 1997, the district has encountered a time of relative harmony and security. Nonetheless, there are still a few difficulties that the district faces, like neediness, joblessness, and ecological debasement.

Chittagong Hill Tracts

Sylhet is a division in the northeastern district of Bangladesh. It is known for its rich green tea gardens, moving slopes, and pleasant cascades. Sylhet is additionally home to the most established tea garden in the subcontinent, Malnicherra Tea Domain.

Sylhet tea garden

Tea gardens have been a part of the Sylhet scene for north of 150 years. The English East India Organization previously acquainted tea development with the district during the nineteenth hundred years. Today, Sylhet is one of the biggest makers of tea in Bangladesh.

There are north of 150 tea gardens in Sylhet, covering an area of more than 150,000 sections of land. The tea gardens are situated in the lower regions of the Himalayas, where the environment and soil are great for tea development.

The most well known tea gardens in Sylhet include:

Malnicherra Tea Home

Lakkatura Tea Nursery

Seven Variety Tea Nursery

Lalakhal Tea Nursery

Evergreen Tea Nursery

Srimangal Tea Nursery

Guests to Sylhet can visit the tea gardens, find out about the tea-production cycle, and test various assortments of tea. Numerous tea plants likewise offer convenience and feasting offices, so guests can remain for the time being and experience the tea garden way of life.

Here are a portion of the things you can do in a Sylhet tea garden:

Go for a stroll through the tea plants and respect the landscape.

Find out about the tea-production process, from culling the passes on to handling the tea.

Test various assortments of tea, including dark tea, green tea, and white tea.

Tea tasting in Sylhet

Visit a tea production line and perceive how tea is handled.

Eat at a tea garden café and partake in a feast with perspectives on the tea gardens.

Remain for the time being at a tea garden lodge and experience the tea garden way of life.

Historical Sites

Bangladesh is a country with a rich and different history, going back more than 5000 years. Thus, there are numerous authentic destinations to be tracked down all through the nation, addressing various societies and periods. thanks

Here are probably the most famous verifiable destinations in Bangladesh:

Lalbagh Post: This incomplete Mughal post in Dhaka was implicit in the seventeenth 100 years by Ruler Azam Shah. It is one of the most famous vacation spots in Bangladesh and is known for its wonderful engineering and gardens.

Lalbagh Post

Ahsan Manzil Historical centre: This previous royal residence of the Nawab of Dhaka inherited the nineteenth 100 years and presently houses a historical centre devoted to the set of experiences and culture of Bangladesh.

Ahsan Manzil Exhibition hall

Public Saints' Landmark: This landmark in Dhaka is committed to the saints of the Bangladesh Freedom Battle of 1971. It is a well known traveller objective and is likewise a position of public journey.

Public Saints' Landmark, Bangladesh

Somapura Mahavihara: This eighth century Buddhist religious community in Paharpur is one of the biggest and most significant Buddhist archeological locales in South Asia. It is an UNESCO World Legacy Site and is available to guests.

Somapura Mahavihara

Tara Masjid: This eighteenth century mosque in Dhaka is known for its lovely star-moulded plan. It is a well known vacationer location and is likewise a position of love for Muslims.

Tara Masjid

Pooped Gambuj Mosque: This fifteenth century mosque in Bagerhat is known for its 60 vaults and is perhaps the biggest mosque on the planet. It is an UNESCO World Legacy Site and is available to guests.

Crapped Gambuj Mosque

Sonargaon: This town on the edges of Dhaka is known for its Mughal-time design and its conventional specialties. It is a famous traveller objective and is likewise a decent spot to find out about the set of experiences and culture of Bangladesh.

Sonargaon, Bangladesh

Mahasthangarh: This archeological site in Bogra is the most established metropolitan settlement in Bangladesh. It traces all the way back to the fourth century BCE and was the capital of the Pundra Realm. It is a famous vacationer location and is likewise a decent spot to find out about the early history of Bangladesh.

Chapter 4. Experience the Cuisine and Dining in Bangladesh

Bangladeshi cooking is a different and delightful mix of impacts from its rich history and geology. The nation's staple food is rice, which is regularly joined by different curries, vegetables, and pickles. Fish is additionally extremely well known, and many dishes are made with new fish from the country's numerous streams and shoreline.

Here are probably the most famous Bangladeshi dishes to attempt:

Biryani: A rice dish cooked with meat, fish, or vegetables and a mix of flavours. Biryani is a must-attempt while visiting Bangladesh, and it's served in pretty much every café the nation over.

Hilsa: A sort of fish that is viewed as a public delicacy in Bangladesh. Hilsa can be cooked in different ways, yet it is most famous when barbecued or broiled.

Khichuri: A rice and lentil dish that is frequently had for breakfast or lunch. Khichuri is a basic yet tasty dish that is ideally suited for those on a careful spending plan.

Pitha: A sort of cake or bread made with rice flour and coconut milk. Pitha is normally eaten during celebrations and festivities, however it can likewise be tracked down in numerous eateries.

Rosogolla: A sweet treat produced using milk and sugar. Rosogolla is a famous treat in Bangladesh and is frequently served at unique events.

In the event that you're searching for a genuinely bona fide Bangladeshi feasting experience, go to one of the numerous road food restaurants or neighbourhood bistros. Here you can track down different conventional dishes at entirely sensible costs. For a more upscale eating experience, there are likewise numerous magnificent eateries in Dhaka and other significant urban communities.

The following are a couple of ways to eat in Bangladesh:

Be ready for zest: Bangladeshi food is known for its strong flavours and liberal utilisation of flavours. On the off chance that you're not used to hot food, make certain to ask your server for suggestions.

Eat with your right hand: It is standard to eat with your right hand in Bangladesh. On the off chance that you're left-given, just switch your fork and blade.

Go ahead and attempt new things: Bangladeshi cooking brings a ton to the table, so make it a point to attempt new dishes. Local people are dependably glad to suggest their top choices.

With its tasty food and cordial individuals, Bangladesh is an extraordinary spot to encounter another culture and cooking. So whenever you're searching for a culinary experience, make certain to add Bangladesh to your rundown.

Traditional Bangladeshi Food

Conventional Bangladeshi food is a flavorful and different cooking that mirrors the country's rich history and culture. Rice is the staple food in Bangladesh, and it is commonly presented with different curries, vegetables, and lentils. Fish is additionally exceptionally famous, and there are a wide range of ways of setting it up.

Here are probably the most famous customary Bangladeshi dishes:

Shorshe Ilish (Hilsa Fish with Mustard Curry): This is an exemplary Bangladeshi dish made with hilsa fish, which is a famous fish in the district. The fish is cooked in a mustard curry sauce that is both tasty and fiery.

Shorshe Ilish (Hilsa Fish with Mustard Curry)

Kacchi Biryani (Lamb Biryani): This is a rice dish made with lamb, rice, and various flavours. It is a famous dish for exceptional events, like weddings and celebrations.

Kacchi Biryani (Sheep Biriyani)

Hamburger Kala Bhuna (Meat Curry): This is a rich and delightful meat curry that is made with various flavours, including onions, garlic, ginger, and yoghurt.

Meat Kala Bhuna (Hamburger Curry)
Bhuna Khichuri with Faint Bhaji (Yellow Rice with Omelet): This is a famous dish for breakfast or lunch. It is made with rice, lentils, and flavours, and it is frequently presented with a broiled omelette.
rumkisgoldenspoon.com
Bhuna Khichuri with Faint Bhaji (Yellow Rice with Omelet)
Sheek Kebab with Naan (Kebab with Flatbread): This is a well known dish for supper or lunch. It is made with ground meat that is prepared with flavours and afterward barbecued. It is frequently presented with naan bread, which is a sort of flatbread.
Sheek Kebab with Naan (Kebab with Flatbread)
Dal (Lentil Soup): This is a well known dish for both lunch and supper. It is made with lentils, flavours, and frequently vegetables. A solid and nutritious dish is likewise truly reasonable.
Dal (Lentil Soup)
Bhorta (Pounded Vegetables with Flavors): This is a well known side dish that is made with various vegetables, like eggplant, potatoes, and tomatoes. The vegetables are crushed and afterward prepared with flavours.
Bhorta (Crushed Vegetables with Flavors)
Fuchka (Seared Pani Puri): This is a famous road food that is made with broiled batter shells that are

loaded up with various fixings, like potatoes, chickpeas, and tamarind sauce.

Fuchka (Broiled Pani Puri)

These are only a couple of the numerous flavorful customary Bangladeshi dishes that you can attempt. Assuming you have the potential chance to visit Bangladesh, make certain to test a portion of the nearby cooking. You won't be frustrated!

Street Food and Local Delicacies

Bangladeshi food brings a ton to the table to its guests. It is a blend of South Asian, Center Eastern, and Mughal impacts, and it is known for its striking flavours and rich flavours.

Bangladesh is likewise known for its dynamic road food scene. From the clamouring roads of Dhaka to the tight paths of Chittagong, you can track down an assortment of flavorful road food to attempt every step of the way.

The following are a couple of the most well known road food and neighbourhood delights in Bangladesh:

Fuchka road food in Bangladesh

Fuchka is a well known road nibble in Bangladesh. It is made with a fresh puri shell loaded up with a combination of pureed potatoes, chickpeas, onions, bean stew, and tamarind chutney. Fuchka is ordinarily presented with a little bowl of hot water to dunk it in.

Jhal Muri road food in Bangladesh

Jhal Muri is another well known Bangladeshi road nibble. It is made with puffed rice, potatoes, onions, peanuts, coriander, and different flavours. Jhal Muri is a tart and zesty dish that is ideal for a light meal in a hurry.

Shingara road food in Bangladesh

Shingara is a Bangladeshi rendition of the samosa. It is a rotisserie baked good loaded up with a combination of flavoured potatoes and onions. Shingara is commonly presented with a chutney or sauce.

Haleem road food in Bangladesh

Haleem is a good stew made with meat, lentils, and flavours. It is a famous dish in Bangladesh throughout the cold weather months.

Biryani road food in Bangladesh

Biryani is a rice dish that is famous all over South Asia. Bangladeshi biryani is normally made with meat, rice, and flavours. A tasty and sweet-smelling dish is ideal for an exceptional event.

Lassi road food in Bangladesh

Lassi is a yoghurt-based drink that is well known in Bangladesh and different parts of South Asia. Lassi can be made either sweet or appetising. Sweet lassi is commonly made with sugar and natural products, while appetising lassi is made with flavours and spices.

Neighbourhood Indulgences

Notwithstanding the famous road food things recorded above, there are various neighbourhood rarities that you can attempt in Bangladesh. The following are a couple of ideas:

Kacchi Biryani is a sluggish cooked biryani that is made with sheep and rice. It is a well known dish during Eid ul-Fitr and other extraordinary events.

Bhuna Khichuri is a good khichuri that is made with meat, lentils, and flavours. It is a famous dish throughout the cold weather months.

Patla Khichuri is a light and invigorating khichuri that is made with rice, lentils, and vegetables. It is a famous dish throughout the late spring months.

Morog Polao is a rice dish that is made with chicken and flavours. It is a famous dish throughout the cold weather months.

Rice with Curry, Vorta, Vaji, and Daal is a customary Bangladeshi dinner. Rice is the fundamental course, and it is normally presented with different curries, vegetables, and lentils.

Dining Etiquette

Eating manners in Bangladesh is an impression of the country's rich culture and customs. Bangladeshis are known for their neighbourliness and liberality, and they invest heavily in imparting their food to other people.

Here are a few hints on feasting behaviour in Bangladesh:

Clean up prior to eating. This is viewed as a noble gesture and tidiness.

Eat with your right hand. The left hand is viewed as messy and is utilised for individual cleanliness errands.

Eat gradually and bite with your mouth shut. It is thought of as discourteous to hurry through your dinner or to make clear commotions while eating.

Try not to begin eating until the most established individual at the table starts. This is a noble gesture.

Take just little divides of food at a time. It is viewed as considerate to complete what you take on your plate.

Try not to pass food around the table. It is viewed as more considerate to take a serving from the fundamental dish and afterward return to your seat to eat.

On the off chance that you are a visitor, it is well mannered to acknowledge a second helping of food, regardless of whether you are not full. This is an indication of appreciation for your host's friendliness.

Leave no food on your plate. This is viewed as inefficient and ill bred.

Thank your host for the dinner before you leave.

Here are a few extra tips:

In the event that you are welcome to a Bangladeshi home for a feast, bringing a little gift is standard. This could be something basic, like blossoms, natural products, or desserts.

Showing up on time for a meal is likewise standard. In the event that you are late, make certain to call or text your host to tell them.

Be ready to eat with your hands. Bangladeshis frequently eat with their hands, and doing likewise is viewed as affable. Nonetheless, in the event that you are not happy eating with your hands, it is completely satisfactory to request utensils.

Chapter 5. Accommodation Options for Bangladesh Visitors

There are an assortment of convenience choices accessible for guests to Bangladesh, contingent upon their financial plan and inclinations. The following are a couple of ideas:

Lavish Inns

Radisson Blu Dhaka Water Nursery: This 5-star inn is situated in the core of Dhaka and offers dazzling perspectives on the city horizon. It includes different conveniences, including a pool, spa, and wellness focus.

Radisson Blu Dhaka Water Nursery

Dish Pacific Sonargaon Dhaka: This 5-star lodging is situated in the upscale Gulshan area of Dhaka and is known for its phenomenal help and conveniences. It includes a pool, spa, wellness focus, and a few eateries

Container Pacific Sonargaon Dhaka

The Westin Dhaka: This 5-star inn is situated in the Gulshan area of Dhaka and offers different conveniences, including a pool, spa, wellness focus, and a few cafés.

Westin Dhaka

Mid-Reach Inns

Inn Elaborate: This 3-star inn is situated in the core of Dhaka and offers agreeable rooms and great help.

Inn Lavish

Inn Shuktara Dhaka: This 3-star lodging is situated in Dhaka and offers different conveniences, including a wellness community, pool, and café.

Inn Shuktara Dhaka

Nagar Valley Inn Ltd.: This 3-star lodging is situated in Srimangal and is an extraordinary choice for those hoping to investigate the tea nurseries of the locale.

Nagar Valley Inn Ltd.

Financial plan Cordial Lodgings and Inns

This 2-star lodging is situated in Dhaka and offers reasonable rooms and a decent area.

The Explorers Cave: This inn is situated in Dhaka and offers an assortment of quarters, beds and confidential rooms. It likewise has a typical region where visitors can mingle and unwind.

Explorers Nook

An insatiable craving for new experiences Inn: This inn is situated in Cox's Bazar and is an extraordinary choice for spending plan explorers. It offers an assortment of residence beds and confidential rooms, as well as a typical region and kitchen.

A chronic desire for new adventures Inn

Homestays and Eco-Hotels

Homestays in Rangamati Slope Region: There are various homestays accessible in the Rangamati Slope Region, which is an extraordinary method for encountering the nearby culture and nature.

Homestays in Rangamati Slope Area

Eco-lodges in the Sundarbans: There are various eco-lodges accessible in the Sundarbans, which is an UNESCO World Legacy Site. These hotels are an incredible method for encountering the exceptional mangrove timberland environment.

Ecolodges in the Sundarbans

While picking convenience in Bangladesh, it is vital to think about your financial plan, inclinations, and the pieces of the country you will visit. In the event that you are remaining in Dhaka, it is ideal to pick an inn in a focal area, like Gulshan, Baridhara, or Banani. On the off chance that you are visiting different pieces of the country, there are an assortment of convenience choices accessible, contingent upon your financial plan and inclinations.

Hotels and Resorts

Bangladesh is a delightful country with a rich culture and history. It is likewise home to various lodgings and resorts, taking care of all spending plans and interests. Here are the absolute most famous lodgings and resorts in Bangladesh:

Ocean Pearl Ocean side Hotel and Spa, Cox's Bazar: This lavish hotel is situated on the world's longest ocean side, Cox's Bazar. It offers staggering perspectives on the Sound of Bengal, as well as various conveniences, including a confidential ocean side, numerous pools, a spa, and a few cafés.

Ocean Pearl Oceanside Retreat and Spa, Cox's Bazar

Dish Pacific Sonargaon Dhaka: This five-star resort is situated in the core of Dhaka, the capital of Bangladesh. It offers extensive and very much selected rooms and suites, as well as different conveniences, including a pool, a wellness community, and a few cafés.

Container Pacific Sonargaon Dhaka

Sea Heaven Lodging and Resort, Cox's Bazar: This family-accommodating hotel is additionally situated on Cox's Bazar ocean side. It offers an assortment of room types, including cabins and estates, as well as various conveniences, including a pool, a children's club, and a few cafés.

Sea Haven Inn and Resort, Cox's Bazar

The Royal residence Extravagance Resort, Cox's Bazar: This lavish hotel is situated on a confidential ocean side in Cox's Bazar. It offers staggering perspectives on the Sound of Bengal, as well as various conveniences, including a confidential ocean side, numerous pools, a spa, and a few cafés.

Castle Extravagance Resort, Cox's Bazar

Amazing Ruler Tea Resort and Golf, Sylhet: This hotel is situated in the rich tea nurseries of Sylhet, in northeastern Bangladesh. It offers an assortment of room types, including bungalows and estates, as well as various conveniences, including a pool, a fairway, and a few cafés.

Fantastic Ruler Tea Resort and Golf, Sylhet

These are only a couple of the numerous lodgings and resorts accessible in Bangladesh. While picking an inn or resort, make certain to think about your spending plan, interests, and the area you need to remain in.

Guesthouses and Homestays

Inn The Charmed, Dhaka. This guesthouse in the core of Dhaka offers agreeable rooms and a cordial air. Visitors can partake in the housetop porch, which offers staggering perspectives on the city.

Lodging The Captivated, Dhaka

Green Leaf Visitor House, Sreemangal. This guesthouse is situated in the delightful tea nation of Sreemangal. It offers extensive rooms and a lavish nursery. Visitors can partake in different exercises, like climbing, trekking, and visiting tea manors.

Green Leaf Visitor House, Sreemangal

Beat Social Visitor House, Cox's Bazar. This guesthouse is situated in the core of Cox's Bazar, the world's longest regular oceanside. It offers reasonable rooms and various social exercises, like film evenings, grills, and oceanside games.

Beat Social Visitor House, Cox's Bazar

Bonorupa Kuakata inn, Kuakata. This guest house is situated near the ocean in Kuakata, a well known traveller destination. It offers agreeable rooms and various conveniences, like a pool, eatery, and bar.

Bonorupa Kuakata inn, Kuakata

Asba Bungalow, Maulvi Bāzār. This bungalow is situated in the town of Maulvi Bāzār, encompassed by lavish green tea manors. It offers a customary Bangladeshi encounter, with basic however agreeable rooms and flavorful home-prepared feasts.

Asba Cabin, Maulvi Bāzār

These are only a couple of the numerous guesthouses and homestays accessible in Bangladesh. While picking a guesthouse or homestay, it is vital to think about your spending plan, area inclinations, and wanted conveniences. It is likewise really smart to pursue audits from different visitors to find out about what's in store.

Camping and Eco-Lodges

Bangladesh is a lovely country with a different scene, including sea shores, slopes, woodlands, and streams. It is likewise home to an assortment of untamed life, including tigers, elephants, and dolphins.

On the off chance that you are searching for a setting up camp or eco-stop insight in Bangladesh, the following are a couple of choices:

Setting up camp

Karnaphuli Eco Town: This camping area is situated in the Chittagong Slope Lots, encompassed by lavish green timberlands and the Karnaphuli Waterway. You can camp in your own tent or lease one from the camping area. There are likewise bamboo cabins accessible for lease.

Karnaphuli Eco Town

Swiss Valley Resort: This retreat is situated in the Sylhet locale of Bangladesh, known for its beautiful excellence and tea gardens. The retreat offers an assortment of setting up camp choices, including tents, cabins, and treehouses.

Swiss Valley Resort

The Headquarters, Bangladesh: This camping area is situated in the Chittagong Slope Plots, close to the town of Bandarban. It offers an assortment of setting up camp choices, including tents, loungers, and bamboo bungalows.

Headquarters, Bangladesh

Ruler Shuk Eco Resort: This hotel is situated on Holy person Martin's Island, a little island in the Sound of Bengal. It offers an assortment of setting up camp choices, including tents, houses, and cabins.

Lord Shuk Eco Resort

Eco-Hotels

DERA Resort and Spa: This retreat is situated in Cox's Bazar, the world's longest solid oceanside. It offers an assortment of eco-accommodating facilities, including estates, bungalows, and treehouses.

DERA Resort and Spa

Rainya Tugun Eco Resort: This hotel is situated in Rangamati, a region in the Chittagong Slope Lots known for its normal magnificence and social legacy. It offers an assortment of eco-accommodating facilities, including houses, cottages, and tents.

Rainya Tugun Eco Resort

Terrific Nuresa Lodging and Resort: This hotel is situated in Cox's Bazar, close to the Inani Ocean side. It offers an assortment of eco-accommodating facilities, including estates, houses, and suites.

Terrific Nuresa Inn and Resort

While picking a setting up camp or eco-stop in Bangladesh, taking into account the accompanying factors is significant:

Location: Would you like to camp in the mountains, around the ocean, or in the backwoods?

Budget: How much would you say you will spend?

Facilities: What sort of offices are essential to you, like latrines, showers, and eateries?

Chapter 6. Transportation Options

Bangladesh has an assortment of transportation choices accessible, including:

Street transport: This is the most widely recognized method of transport in Bangladesh, and incorporates different vehicles like transports, taxis, auto-carts, and carts. Transports are the most well known type of really long travel, and there are various different transport organisations working all through the country. Cabs and auto-carts are a decent choice for more limited trips, yet it is essential to settle on a cost with the driver prior to getting in. Carts are the most conventional type of transport in Bangladesh, and are an effective method for getting around in blocked regions.

Rail transport: Bangladesh Railroad works as an organisation of trains that associate the significant urban communities and towns in the country. Trains are a somewhat sluggish and awkward method of transport, however they are likewise the least expensive.

Water transport: Bangladesh has a huge organisation of streams and channels, and water transport is a well known method for getting around, particularly in rustic regions. There are various sorts of watercraft accessible, including ships, boats, and dispatches.

Air transport: Bangladesh has various homegrown and global air terminals. Air travel is the quickest method for getting around the nation, yet it is additionally the most costly.

The best method of transport for you will rely upon your financial plan, your time requirements, and the distance you are voyaging.

Here are a few extra ways to pick the correct method of transport in Bangladesh:

In the event that you are going on a strict financial plan, transports and trains are the most ideal choices.

Assuming you are voyaging significant distances, air travel is the quickest method for getting around.

On the off chance that you are going in a blocked city, carts are an effective method for getting around.

On the off chance that you are going in a rustic region, water transport is a well known choice.

On the off chance that you are going with a ton of gear, taxis are the most ideal choice.

Getting Around Bangladesh

Bangladesh has a decent transportation framework, with various choices accessible to voyagers.

Air: Bangladesh has two worldwide air terminals, Shahjalal Global Air terminal in Dhaka and Osmani Worldwide Air terminal in Sylhet. There are likewise various homegrown air terminals, interfacing significant urban communities and traveller objections.

Rail: Bangladesh has an exhaustive rail organisation, with trains interfacing every significant city and towns. Trains are a famous and reasonable method for going around the nation, however they can be packed and slow.

Bus: Transports are the most well-known type of transportation in Bangladesh, with administrations associating all pieces of the country. Transports can be packed and awkward, yet they are additionally the least expensive method for voyaging.

Rickshaw: Carts are a well known method for getting around Dhaka and other significant urban communities. They are moderately reasonable and can be utilised to travel brief distances.

Taxi: Taxis are accessible in all significant urban communities and traveller objections. They are more costly than different types of transportation, yet they are likewise more agreeable and helpful.

Water: Bangladesh has an organisation of waterways and channels, which can be utilised to head out to many pieces of the country. Ships and boats are accessible, and can be a grand method for voyaging.

Here are a few ways to get around Bangladesh:

Prepare for time: This will assist you with abstaining from getting lost or with nothing to do.

Be ready for swarms: All types of transportation in Bangladesh can be packed, particularly during top hours.

Know about your environmental elements: This is particularly significant while taking cabs or carts.

Arrange costs: Costs for transportation in Bangladesh are frequently debatable, particularly for carts and taxicabs.

Show restraint: Traffic can be weighty in Bangladesh, and transports and trains can be deferred.

By and large, getting around Bangladesh is moderately simple and reasonable. There are an assortment of transportation choices accessible, and explorers can pick the one that best suits their necessities and spending plan.

DOMESTIC FLIGHTS AND TRAIN

Homegrown flights and trains are the two most well known ways of going between significant urban communities in Bangladesh. Flights are the quickest choice, however preparations are more reasonable and offer a more beautiful excursion.

Homegrown trips in Bangladesh

There are five homegrown aircrafts in Bangladesh:

Biman Bangladesh Carriers

NovoAir

US-Bangla Carriers

Official Aviation routes

Air Astra

These carriers offer trips to all significant urban areas in Bangladesh, including Dhaka, Chittagong, Sylhet, Cox's Bazar, and Rajshahi.

Flight times

The flight time among Dhaka and other significant urban areas in Bangladesh is ordinarily somewhere in the range of 30 and an hour. For instance, the flight time from Dhaka to Chittagong is around 45 minutes.

Flight costs

The expense of homegrown trips in Bangladesh fluctuates relying upon the aircraft, the course, and the season. Be that as it may, flights are by and large reasonable, particularly when contrasted with global flights. For instance, a one-way departure from Dhaka to Chittagong normally costs around $50-$70.

Homegrown trains in Bangladesh

Bangladesh Railroad works as a complete organisation of trains that interface every significant city and towns in the country. There are three kinds of trains in Bangladesh:

Intercity trains: These trains are the quickest and most agreeable choice, and they offer an assortment of seating classes, including cooled seats and sleeper vehicles.

Mail trains: These trains are slower than intercity trains, however they are likewise more reasonable. They offer an assortment of seating classes, including cooled seats and non-cooled seats.

Neighbourhood trains: These trains are the slowest and least expensive choice, and they commonly just deal with non-cooled seats.

Train times

The train time among Dhaka and other significant urban communities in Bangladesh changes relying upon the kind of train and the course. Be that as it may, trains are for the most part slower than flights. For instance, the train venture from Dhaka to Chittagong requires around 10 hours.

Train costs

The expense of homegrown trains in Bangladesh is entirely reasonable. For instance, a one-way ticket on an intercity train from Dhaka to Chittagong commonly costs around $10-$20.

Which choice is best for you?

The most ideal way to go between significant urban areas in Bangladesh relies upon your spending plan and your inclinations. In the event that you are searching for the quickest choice, flying is the most ideal decision. Be that as it may, assuming you are on a limited spending plan or you need to partake in a more picturesque excursion, then taking the train is a decent choice.

Here is a table that looks at homegrown flights and trains in Bangladesh:

Factor	Flights	Trains
Speed	Faster	Slower
Cost	More expensive	Less costly
Comfort	More comfortable	Less agreeable
Picturesque value	Less scenic	More beautiful

Local Transport Tips

Bangladesh has an assortment of neighbourhood transport choices, including transports, trains, carts, and taxicabs. Here are a few hints to assist you with getting around securely and helpfully:

Buses: Transports are the most well known type of public transportation in Bangladesh. They are moderately reasonable and can take you to most pieces of the country. In any case, transports can be packed and awkward, particularly during busy times. To keep away from the groups, attempt to go beyond top hours. You can likewise buy a ticket for a higher-class transport, which will be more open and less swarmed.

Trains: Trains are one more famous method for voyaging significant distances in Bangladesh. They are more agreeable than transports, yet they can likewise be more costly. Train timetables can be sporadic, so reserving your tickets in advance is significant.

Rickshaws: Carts are a tomfoolery and helpful method for getting around brief distances in Bangladesh. There are two sorts of carts: cycle carts and mechanised carts. Cycle carts are all the more harmless to the ecosystem, however they can be increasingly slow tiring for the driver. Mechanised carts are quicker, however they can be more costly and boisterous.

Taxis: Taxis are the most costly type of nearby transportation in Bangladesh, however they are likewise the most advantageous. Cabs can be found at air terminals, train stations, and significant lodgings. You can likewise flag down a taxi in the city, yet make certain to settle on a cost with the driver prior to getting in.

Here are a few extra ways to involve nearby transportation in Bangladesh:

Be ready to arrange: Arranging costs with cart and cab drivers in Bangladesh is normal. Begin by offering a lower cost than what you will pay, and be ready to leave in the event that you can't agree.

Know about your environmental elements: Neighbourhood traffic can be tumultuous, so it is vital to know about your environmental factors while utilising public transportation. Watch out for going across the road, and try not to stand excessively near the edge of the street.

Be aware of nearby traditions: Bangladeshis are for the most part well disposed and inviting individuals. Notwithstanding, it is critical to be conscious of their traditions and customs. For instance, ladies ought to abstain from wearing revealing clothing.

Chapter 7. Culture and Traditions

Bangladesh is a country with a rich and varied culture, impacted by its long history and multicultural populace. Most of the populace is Muslim, yet there are likewise critical Hindu, Buddhist, and Christian minorities. This variety is reflected in the nation's celebrations, food, music, dance, and craftsmanship.

Here are the absolute most famous social and conventional parts of Bangladesh:

Clothing: The customary apparel of Bangladesh is the sari for ladies and the lungi for men. In any case, individuals in metropolitan regions likewise wear Western apparel.

Food: Bangladeshi cooking is known for its utilisation
of flavours and its accentuation on rice and fish. Probably the most well known dishes incorporate biryani, pulao, kebabs, and curry.

Music: Bangladeshi music is a mix of conventional and present day impacts. The absolute most well known kinds incorporate people music, traditional music, and popular music.

Dance: Bangladeshi dance is likewise a mix of conventional and current impacts. The absolute most well known moves incorporate the Jatra, the Kathakali, and the Manipuri.

Art: Bangladeshi workmanship is known for its brilliant varieties and many-sided plans. Probably the most famous artistic expressions incorporate Nakshi Kantha, stoneware, and painting.

Notwithstanding these overall social perspectives, there are likewise various explicit customs that are seen in Bangladesh. For instance, it is standard to welcome seniors with deference and to offer them food and beverages. Taking off one's shoes prior to entering a mosque or temple is likewise standard

Here are the absolute most famous celebrations in Bangladesh:

Eid al-Fitr: This celebration denotes the finish of Ramadan, the Muslim blessed month of fasting.

Eid al-Adha: This celebration honours the ability of the Prophet Ibrahim to forfeit his child Ismail as a demonstration of dutifulness to God.

Durga Puja: This Hindu celebration praises the triumph of the goddess Durga over the devil Mahishasura.

Christmas: This Christian celebration praises the introduction of Jesus Christ.

Pahela Baishakh: This is the Bengali New Year celebration, which is commended by individuals, everything being equal.

Festivals and Celebrations

Bangladesh is a nation of celebrations and festivities. With a rich and varied culture, there is something for everybody to appreciate over time. Here is a rundown of probably the most well known celebrations and festivities in Bangladesh:

Pohela Boishakh (Bengali New Year): Pohela Boishakh is the Bengali New Year and is praised on the main day of the Bengali month of Baishakh (generally in April). It is a public occasion and is praised with extraordinary energy and pomp. Individuals wear new garments, visit sanctuaries and mosques, and trade good tidings with loved ones. There are likewise numerous widespread developments and exhibitions hung on this day.

Pohela Boishakh celebration in Bangladesh

Ekushey February (Worldwide Mother Language Day): Ekushey February is commended on February 21st to recognize the suffering of the people who passed on fighting the burden of Urdu as the public language of East Pakistan in 1952. It is a public occasion and is seen with incredible gravity and regard. Individuals give proper respect to the language saints at different remembrances and hold rallies and parades to request language privileges for all.

Ekushey February celebration in Bangladesh

Autonomy Day (Walk 26th): Autonomy Day is praised on Spring 26th to celebrate the announcement of Bangladesh's freedom from Pakistan in 1971. It is a public occasion and is commended with incredible enthusiasm and intensity. Individuals fly the Bangladeshi banner, sing enthusiastic tunes, and go to marches and different occasions.

Freedom Day celebration in Bangladesh

Triumph Day (December sixteenth): Triumph Day is praised on December sixteenth to remember the triumph of the Bangladeshi freedom powers over the Pakistani armed force in 1971. It is a public occasion and is praised with incredible euphoria and festivity. Individuals fly the Bangladeshi banner, sing enthusiastic tunes, and go to marches and different occasions.

Triumph Day celebration in Bangladesh

Eid-ul-Fitr and Eid-ul-Azha: Eid-ul-Fitr and Eid-ul-Azha are the two most significant Muslim celebrations. Eid-ul-Fitr marks the finish of the fasting month of Ramadan, while Eid-ul-Azha remembers the readiness of the Prophet Ibrahim to forfeit his child Ismail as a demonstration of submission to God. The two celebrations are commended with incredible intensity and excitement. Individuals wear new garments, visit mosques, and trade gifts with loved ones. There are likewise numerous exceptional dishes ready and consumed during these celebrations.

EidulFitr celebration in Bangladesh

Durga Puja: Durga Puja is the main Hindu celebration in Bangladesh. A ten-day celebration commends the triumph of the goddess Durga over the evil spirit Mahishasura. On the 10th day of the celebration, the symbols of Durga are submerged in waterways and lakes in a vivid parade.

Durga Puja celebration in Bangladesh

Christmas: Christmas is praised by Christians in Bangladesh on December 25th. It is a public occasion and is praised with extraordinary delight and party. Individuals adorn their homes and places of worship with Christmas trees and lights, and trade presents with loved ones. There are likewise numerous exceptional occasions and exhibitions hung on this day.

Christmas celebration in Bangladesh

Notwithstanding these significant celebrations, there are likewise numerous different celebrations and festivities held all through the year in Bangladesh. These include:

Basanta Utsab (Spring Celebration)

Nabanna Utsab (New Reap Celebration)

Poush Mela (Winter Fair)

Baul Mela (Baul Celebration)

Weddings

Other strict celebrations like Buddha Purnima (Buddhist celebration),
Janmashtami (Hindu celebration), and Magha Puja (Buddhist celebration)
Social celebrations like the Bengal Unique Culture Celebration, Cinemaking Worldwide Film Celebration, Dhaka Celebration, and Dhaka Craftsmanship Highest point.

Art, Music, and Dance

Bangladesh has a rich and energetic culture, and its specialty, music, and dance are no exemption. The country's creative practices date back hundreds of years, and have been impacted by various societies, including Hinduism, Buddhism, Islam, and the native people groups of the district.

Music

Bangladeshi music can be extensively partitioned into three classes: traditional, society, and present day. Old style music depends on the old Indian melodic practice, and is portrayed by its perplexing tunes and rhythms. Society music is more assorted, and mirrors the country's rich social legacy. Probably the most famous types of people's music incorporate , , jari, sari, marfati, and baul. Present day music in Bangladesh is a blend of customary and Western impacts, and incorporates types like pop, rock, and combination.

Probably the most renowned Bangladeshi performers include:

Rabindranath Tagore: A Nobel laureate writer and author, Tagore is viewed as the dad of Bangladeshi music. His tunes are still generally sung and appreciated today.

Kazi Nazrul Islam: One more Public Writer of Bangladesh, Nazrul Islam was a productive writer of enthusiastic tunes and psalms. His music is known for its strong tunes and blending verses.

Alauddin Khan: An eminent sitar player, Khan is viewed as one of the best old style performers ever. He was likewise the educator of Ravi Shankar.

Ayub Bachchu: A trailblazer of Bangladeshi exciting music, Bachchu was known for his vivacious live exhibitions and his unmistakable way of singing.

James: A famous pop vocalist and lyricist, James is one of the best Bangladeshi performers ever.

Dance.

Bangladeshi dance is likewise different, and incorporates an assortment of old style, society, and ancestral structures. Traditional dance structures, for example, kathakali and bharatanatyam are well known all through the subcontinent, yet Bangladesh likewise has its own novel native moves. Probably the most famous types of society dance incorporate the , baul, manipuri, and snake moves. Each structure communicates a specific part of mutual life and is moved on unambiguous events.

Craftsmanship

Bangladeshi craftsmanship is likewise impacted by the country's rich social legacy. Customary Bangladeshi fine arts incorporate artistic creation, model, stoneware, and materials. The nation is likewise home to various contemporary specialists who are exploring different avenues regarding new structures and styles.

The absolute most well known Bangladeshi specialists include:

SM Ruler: A famous painter, stone worker, and ceramist, Ruler is viewed as one of the main Bangladeshi specialists of the twentieth 100 years. His work is known for its striking utilisation of variety and its investigation of subjects like personality and civil rights.

Kanak Chanpa Chakma: A famous painter and printmaker, Chakma is known for her vivid and expressive works that frequently portray the existences of native ladies.

Qayyum Chowdhury: A prestigious painter and stone worker, Chowdhury is known for his theoretical works that frequently investigate topics like otherworldliness and the human condition.

Shahabuddin Ahmed: A prestigious painter and stone worker, Ahmed is known for his reasonable and frequently graceful portrayals of day to day existence in Bangladesh.

Local Transport Tips

Language and correspondence are fundamental parts of Bangladeshi culture. The authority language of Bangladesh is Bangla, otherwise called Bengali. It is spoken by more than 98% of the populace and is written in its own content, derived from that of Sanskrit. Bangla has a rich scholarly custom, going back more than 1,000 years.

Notwithstanding Bangla, there are various different dialects spoken in Bangladesh, including English, Hindi, Urdu, and Chakma. English is broadly utilised in government, schooling, and business. Hindi and Urdu are spoken by minorities, like the Biharis and the Rohingya. Chakma is a Tibeto-Burman language spoken by the Chakma nation in the Chittagong Slope Lots.

Bangladeshis are for the most part circuitous communicators. They will generally stay away from head on a conflict and may utilise code words or indirect language to offer their viewpoints or solicitations. It is vital to know about this social contrast while speaking with Bangladeshis, as immediate or emphatic language might be seen as discourteous.

Here are a few ways to discuss really with Bangladeshis:

Be amiable and conscious.

Utilise circuitous language while offering viewpoints or solicitations.

Try not to utilise solid or angry language.

Be patient and understanding. It might require an investment to comprehend Bangladeshi culture and correspondence style.

Here are a few normal Bangladeshi expressions and good tidings:

Namaskar (Hindu hello)

Salaam alaikum (Muslim hello)

Khoda hafez (Muslim goodbye)

acho? (How are you?)

Valo achi, ami (I'm well.)

Apni kemon achen? (How are you? (formal))

Aapni valo achen (I'm well. (formal))

Dhanyabঃাদ (Much obliged)

Aapni shongko (The pleasure is all mine).

Chapter 8. Outdoors and Recreation Activities in Bangladesh

Bangladesh is a country with a rich and varied scene, from the snow-covered heaps of the Chittagong Slope Lots to the perfect seashores of Cox's Market. This makes it an extraordinary spot to partake in an assortment of outside and entertainment exercises.

The following are a couple of ideas:

Journeying and Climbing

The Chittagong Slope Plots are home to the absolute most gorgeous and testing climbing trails in Bangladesh. Here, you can travel across lavish rainforests, move up to cascades, and visit distant towns.

pathfriend-bd.com

Journeying in Chittagong Slope Parcels, Bangladesh

Famous journeying objections include:

Sajek Valley: This valley is home to the most elevated point in Bangladesh, Keokradong top, as well as the Sajek cascade.

Rangamati: This town is encircled by slopes and lakes, and there are many travelling trails to browse.

Kaptai Lake: This lake is encircled by slopes and woodlands, and there are a few journeying trails that offer dazzling perspectives.

In the event that you're searching for a really difficult climb, you can attempt the trip to the highest point of Mount Keokradong. This is a two-day journey that takes you through probably the most remote and lovely pieces of the Chittagong Slope Lots.

Birding

Bangladesh is home to north of 600 types of birds, making it an incredible spot for birdwatching. Probably the best places to see birds include:

Sunderbans Public Park: This mangrove timberland is home to an assortment of bird animal types, including the jeopardised Regal Bengal tiger.

Kaptai Lake: This lake is a famous spot for transitory birds, like ducks and geese.

Tanguar Haor: This wetland region is home to an assortment of bird animal groups, including waterbirds and raptors.

On the off chance that you're keen on birding, you can enlist a nearby aide who can assist you with recognizing the best birds.

Boat Visits

Bangladesh has a huge organisation of streams and waterways, making it an incredible spot to take a boat visit. You can visit towns, see untamed life, and partake in the landscape.

Well known boat visit objections include:

Sunderbans Public Park: Take a boat visit through the mangrove woodland to see the Imperial Bengal tiger, crocodiles, and other untamed life.

Tanguar Haor: Take a boat visit through the wetland region to see waterbirds, raptors, and other natural life.

Karnaphuli Waterway: Take a boat visit through the Karnaphuli Waterway to see the Chittagong Extension and different milestones.

Boat visit in Sunderbans Public Park, Bangladesh

Fishing

Bangladesh is an extraordinary spot to go fishing, with an assortment of fish animal categories to browse. You can fish in streams, channels, lakes, and the ocean.

The absolute best places to fish include:

Sunderbans Public Park: Fish for an assortment of fish animal types, including catfish, prawns, and crabs.

Tanguar Haor: Fish for an assortment of fish animal varieties, including carp, catfish, and prawns.

Cox's Market: Fish for an assortment of fish animal types, including fish, mackerel, and pomfret.

In the event that you're keen on fishing, you can enlist a neighbourhood guide who can assist you with tracking down the best places to fish and the best methods to utilise.

Sea shores

Bangladesh has a long shoreline with numerous lovely sea shores. The absolute most well known sea shores include:

Cox's Marketplace: This is the longest ocean side on the planet and is a well known spot for swimming, sunbathing, and surfing.

Kuakata: This ocean side is known for its brilliant sand and clear water.

St. Martin's Island: This coral island is known for its white sand sea shores and completely clear water.

Cox's Marketplace Oceanside, Bangladesh

Untamed life Review

Bangladesh is home to an assortment of untamed life, including the Illustrious Bengal tiger, elephants, dolphins, and crocodiles. The absolute best places to see natural life include:

Sunderbans Public Park: This mangrove timberland is home to the Illustrious Bengal tiger, crocodiles, and other natural life.

Tanguar Haor: This wetland region is home to an assortment of bird animal types, as well as dolphins and crocodiles.

Cox's Market: This ocean side is a well known spot for whale watching.

Adventure Tourism

Bangladesh is a country with a different scene, offering an assortment of experiences that open doors to the travel industry. From the world's biggest mangrove woods to the longest regular oceanside, there is something for everybody in Bangladesh.

Here are the absolute most well known experience the travel industry exercises in Bangladesh:

Sundarbans mangrove woods Bangladesh

The Sundarbans is an UNESCO World Legacy Site and the world's biggest mangrove woods. It is home to an assortment of untamed life, including the Bengal tiger, dolphins, crocodiles, and north of 400 types of birds. Guests can take boat voyages through the woods, go on directed strolls, and, surprisingly, camp for the time being.

Cox's Bazar oceanside Bangladesh

Cox's Bazar ocean side is the world's longest normal oceanside, extending for more than 120 kilometres. It is a well known spot for swimming, sunbathing, and water sports like surfing and fly skiing. Guests can likewise go on boat outings to local islands and watch dolphins.

Lawachara Public Park Bangladesh

Lawachara Public Park is a rainforest situated in the Sylhet division of Bangladesh. It is home to an assortment of untamed life, including elephants, monkeys, and panthers. Guests can go on journeys across the timberland, visit cascades, and take boat voyages through the streams.

Sreemangal tea gardens Bangladesh

Sreemangal is the tea capital of Bangladesh. Guests can take voyages through the tea gardens, find out about the tea-production interaction, and even sample various kinds of tea. There are likewise amazing open doors for journeying and setting up camp in the encompassing slopes.

Chittagong Slope Plots Bangladesh

The Chittagong Slope Plots is a precipitous district in southeastern Bangladesh. It is home to an assortment of ethnic minority gatherings, each with its own extraordinary culture and customs. Guests can go on journeys to ancestral towns, visit Buddhist sanctuaries, and go on boat outings down the waterways.

Notwithstanding these famous exercises, there are an assortment of other experience the travel industry valuable open doors accessible in Bangladesh, for example,

Journeying to cascades and mountain tops

Boating and kayaking on waterways

Going through tea nurseries and towns

Birdwatching in the Sundarbans and different wetlands

Fishing in the waterways and seaside waters

Setting up camp in the public stops and backwoods Bangladesh is a somewhat reasonable country to visit, and there are various visit administrators that proposition experience the travel industry bundles. The best opportunity to visit Bangladesh to experience the travel industry is throughout the cold weather months (October to Spring), when the weather conditions are gentle and dry.

Wildlife and Birdwatching

Bangladesh is a little country in South Asia, however it is home to a noteworthy variety of untamed life and birds. The nation has 17 public parks, 20 untamed life safe-havens, and one exceptional biodiversity preservation region. These safeguarded regions give natural surroundings to a great many animal types, including the Bengal tiger, Asian elephant, Irrawaddy dolphin, estuarine crocodile, and fishing feline.

Estuarine crocodile, Bangladesh

Bangladesh is likewise a significant bird watching destination, with north of 700 types of birds kept in the country. Of these, around 320 are transitory birds, showing up generally from Mongolia, China, Tibet, and Russia during the Northern Half of the globe winter. Probably the most famous bird watching spots in Bangladesh include:

Sundarbans: The Sundarbans is an UNESCO World Legacy Site and the biggest mangrove backwoods on the planet. It is home to many birds, including the Bengal florican, more prominent assistant stork, and hooded pitta.

Sundarbans, Bangladesh

Sangu Matamuhuri: Sangu Matamuhuri is a remote timberland in southeastern Bangladesh. It is home to various interesting and imperilled bird species, like the extraordinary hornbill, wreathed hornbill, and green-charged malkoha.

Sangu Matamuhuri, Bangladesh

Kaptai Public Park: Kaptai Public Park is a lake-based public park in southeastern Bangladesh. It is home to various waterbirds, for example, the lesser whistling duck, brush duck, and dim headed fish falcon.

Kaptai Public Park, Bangladesh

Lawachara Public Park: Lawachara Public Park is a rainforest public park in northeastern Bangladesh. It is home to various bird species that are not tracked down somewhere else in the country, like the red-headed trogon, blue-whiskery honey bee eater, and dark breasted parrotbill.

Lawachara Public Park, Bangladesh

In the event that you are keen on untamed life and birdwatching, Bangladesh is an extraordinary spot to visit. With its different natural surroundings and bountiful untamed life, the nation brings something to the table for everybody.

River Cruises

Bangladesh is a place that is known for waterways, with north of 700 streams mismatching the country. This makes waterway cruising one of the most outstanding ways of investigating the nation and its rich culture and legacy.

There are an assortment of waterway travels accessible in Bangladesh, going from brief road trips to longer multi-day travels. Probably the most well known waterway voyage objections include:

Sundarbans: The Sundarbans is a huge mangrove woodland that is home to the Illustrious Bengal tiger. Stream travels to the Sundarbans offer guests the opportunity to see these lofty animals very close, as well as other untamed life like crocodiles, dolphins, and monkeys.

Sundarbans Stream Voyage Bangladesh

Dhaka: Dhaka is the capital of Bangladesh and a clamouring city. Stream travels in Dhaka offer guests an extraordinary point of view of the city and its kin. Travellers ordinarily withdraw from Sadarghat, the principal stream port in Dhaka, and pass by notorious tourist spots, for example, the Ahsan Manzil, the Lalbagh Post, and the Dhakeshwari Sanctuary.

Dhaka Stream Journey Bangladesh

Sonargaon: Sonargaon is a memorable town situated around 30 kilometres from Dhaka. It is known for its customary expressions and specialties, including earthenware, materials, and metalwork. Waterway travels to Sonargaon regularly incorporate stops at nearby towns to find out about the town's rich culture and legacy.

Sonargaon Stream Journey Bangladesh

Notwithstanding these well known objections, waterway travels are likewise accessible to different pieces of Bangladesh, like Khulna, Barisal, and Sylhet.

Stream travels in Bangladesh ordinarily offer different conveniences, including agreeable lodges, cafés, and sundecks. A few travels likewise incorporate installed diversion, like social exhibitions and unrecorded music.

Cost of Waterway Travels in Bangladesh

The expense of waterway travels in Bangladesh changes relying upon the length of the voyage, the sort of lodge, and the season. Nonetheless, waterway travels are by and large entirely reasonable, particularly when contrasted with different regions of the planet.

For instance, a one-day stream journey to the Sundarbans commonly costs around $100 per individual. A two-day voyage to Sonargaon normally costs around $200 per individual. What's more, a four-day voyage to Khulna and Barisal ordinarily costs around $500 per individual.

Ways to book a Waterway Voyage in Bangladesh

The following are a couple of ways to book a waterway voyage in Bangladesh:

Book your voyage ahead of time, particularly on the off chance that you are going during top season (December to February).

Think about costs from various visit administrators prior to booking.

Make a point to pursue the agreements of your voyage cautiously prior to booking.

Get some information about the conveniences that are remembered for your voyage charge.

Pack light, as you will have restricted space in your lodge.

Bring sunscreen, bug repellent, and a cap, as the weather conditions can be sweltering and sticky.

Be ready for blackouts and different burdens.

Waterway travels offer an interesting and extraordinary method for investigating Bangladesh. With its reasonable costs and assortment of schedules, there is a waterway voyage to suit each financial plan and interest.

Chapter 9. Safety and Travel Tips

Security Tips in Bangladesh

Know about your environmental elements and avoid potential risk against trivial robbery, particularly in jam-packed regions. Pickpocketing and sack grabbing are normal, so keep your resources near you and try not to convey a lot of money.

Be cautious while going across the road. Traffic can be tumultuous and walkers frequently need to avoid vehicles, all things considered.

Try not to travel solo around evening time, particularly in new regions. On the off chance that you should travel solo, take a taxi or ride-flagging down help from a legitimate organisation.

Be aware of neighbourhood customs and customs. Bangladesh is a Muslim-larger part country, so it is critical to dress humbly and keep away from public presentations of warmth.

Know about the political circumstance and keep away from enormous social affairs and fights. Bangladesh has a past filled with political flimsiness, so it is essential to be educated about the most recent turns of events and to stay away from circumstances that could seriously jeopardise you.

Travel Tips in Bangladesh

The best chance to visit Bangladesh is throughout the cold weather months (November to February), when the weather conditions are gentle and radiant. The storm season (June to September) can bring weighty rains and flooding, so trying not to go during this time is ideal.

Bangladesh is a somewhat reasonable country to visit. Notwithstanding, it is essential to plan carefully, as expenses can differ contingent upon your movement style.

There are an assortment of convenience choices accessible in Bangladesh, from spending plan guesthouses to lavish lodgings. It is critical to book your convenience ahead of time, particularly assuming that you are going during the pinnacle season.

Bangladesh is a somewhat simple country to get around. There are an assortment of transportation choices accessible, including transports, trains, taxicabs, and ride-flagging down administrations.

Bangladesh has a rich culture and history. There are various sanctuaries, mosques, and other authentic locales that merit visiting. The nation is likewise home to various normal attractions, for example, the Sundarbans mangrove timberland and the Chittagong Slope Parcels.

Here are a few extra tips for explorers to Bangladesh:

Become familiar with a couple of fundamental Bengali expressions. This will assist you with speaking with local people and get around more without any problem.

Be ready to deal while shopping. Bartering is normal in Bangladesh, so make it a point to deal with sellers.

Attempt the nearby food. Bangladesh has a tasty and fluctuating cooking style. Make certain to attempt a portion of the well known dishes, like biryani, kebabs, and fish curry.

Be patient and understanding. Bangladesh is a non-industrial nation, so things may not generally chug along as expected. Be patient and understanding with local people, and partake in your time in this gorgeous and entrancing country.

Health and Safety Precautions

Bangladesh is a non-industrial nation with various wellbeing and security challenges. It is critical to know about these moves and avoid potential risk to remain protected and sound.

General Wellbeing Safety measures

Receive any available immunisation shots: Ensure you are modern on your immunizations in general, including those for hepatitis A and B, typhoid, cholera, and Japanese encephalitis.

Hydrate: Try not to drink regular water, as it could be defiled.
Clean up regularly: Use cleanser and water to clean up prior to eating, in the wake of utilising the washroom, and subsequent to dealing with crude meat or poultry.
Be cautious about what you eat: Try not to eat crude leafy foods, and ensure that meat and poultry are cooked completely.
Use sunscreen and bug repellent: Shield yourself from the sun and mosquitoes by utilising sunscreen and bug repellent with DEET.
Wellbeing Insurances
Know about your environmental factors: Bangladesh can be a packed and turbulent nation, so it is vital to know about your environmental factors and play it safe to try not to be pickpocketed or robbed.
Try not to walk alone around evening time: It is ideal to try not to walk alone around evening time, particularly in new regions.
Be cautious while going across the road: Traffic in Bangladesh can be turbulent and perilous. Be cautious while going across the road, and

consistently utilise the crosswalk in the event that there is one.

Know about the climate: Bangladesh is inclined to cataclysmic events like typhoons and floods. Know about the weather conditions estimate and play it safe if vital.

Extra Insurances for Voyagers to Bangladesh

Register with your government office or department: This will assist them with reaching you in the event of a crisis.

Buy travel protection: Travel protection can safeguard you against surprising occasions like lost gear, health related crises, and dropped flights.

Gain proficiency with a couple of essential Bengali expressions: This will assist you with speaking with local people and get around more without any problem.

Word related Wellbeing and Wellbeing

Assuming you are working in Bangladesh, it is essential to know about the word related security and wellbeing perils that might be available in your work environment. A few normal dangers include:

Electrical risks: Electrical wiring in Bangladesh is frequently hazardous, and there is a high gamble of electric shock.

Fire perils: Structures in Bangladesh are frequently inadequately built and packed, which expands the gamble of flames.

Synthetic perils: Labourers in certain ventures, for example, pieces of clothing assembling and tanneries, might be presented to unsafe synthetic substances.

Actual perils: Labourers in numerous ventures might be presented to actual risks like commotion, residue, and vibration.

Assuming you are working in Bangladesh, it means quite a bit to play it safe to shield yourself from these dangers. A portion of the things you can do include:

Wear proper individual defensive gear (PPE): This might incorporate gloves, goggles, covers, and hard caps.

Know about the risks in your work environment: Converse with your boss or different labourers about the risks that are available, and how to stay away from them.

Report any risks to your boss: Assuming you see a danger, report it to your boss with the goal that it tends to be fixed.

On the off chance that you are harmed or wiped out in Bangladesh, it is critical to quickly look for clinical consideration. There are various clinics and facilities in Bangladesh, however some might be of preferable quality over others. It is really smart to do some exploration before you travel to

Bangladesh so you know where to go for clinical assistance assuming you want it.

Local Customs and Etiquette

Bangladesh is a different country with a rich culture and history. It is critical to be deferential to neighbourhood customs and decorum while visiting Bangladesh, to try not to cause offence.

Here are a few general tips:

Dress humbly. All kinds of people ought to dress humbly in Bangladesh. This implies abstaining from uncovering clothing, for example, shorts, tank tops, and low profile dresses. Ladies may likewise need to cover their heads with a scarf, particularly in provincial regions.

Be conscious of older folks. Bangladeshis put a high value on regard for elderly folks. While hello a senior, it is standard to bow marginally or place your hands together before your chest. You ought to likewise try not to talk noisily or intruding on a senior.

Utilise your right hand. Bangladeshis utilise their right hand for most errands, including eating, shaking hands, and passing articles. Involving your left hand for these things is viewed as inconsiderate.

Try not to show public presentations of fondness. Bangladeshis are for the most part moderate and don't endorse public presentations of friendship, like kissing or embracing.

Show restraint. Bangladeshis can be exceptionally persistent individuals, yet it is critical to recollect that things may not necessarily in every case occur as fast as you are utilised to. Be patient and understanding, and you will be compensated with a warm and inviting experience.

Here are a few extra tips for explicit circumstances:

Greetings: While hello somebody in Bangladesh, it is standard to say "Assalamualaikum" (harmony arrive). On the off chance that you are not Muslim, you can essentially say "Hi" or "Namaste".

Gifts: In the event that you are welcome to a Bangladeshi home, it is standard to bring a little gift, like roses, desserts, or natural products. Try not to open your gift before the provider.

Dining: Bangladeshis regularly eat with their right hands. In the event that you are not happy eating with your hands, you can request utensils. Completing the food on your plate is all viewed as amenable.

Business: Bangladeshi business culture is by and large formal. It is essential to dress expertly and to be on time for gatherings. While shaking hands, make certain to utilise your right hand.

By following these tips, you can recognize Bangladeshi culture and behaviour, and guarantee that you have a positive and charming involvement with this delightful country.

Emergency Contacts

Here are some significant crisis contacts in Bangladesh:

Public Crisis Administration: 999

Police: 112

Rescue vehicle: 125

Fire Administration: 119

Hostile to abducting hotline: 165

You can likewise call the accompanying numbers for explicit sorts of help:

Public Helpline Community for Savagery against Ladies and Youngsters: 109

Kid Helpline: 1098

Wellbeing Call Centre: 16263

Weather conditions Figure: 106

BIWTA Helpline: 16237

Tottho Apa at Public Ladies' Association: 16466

Sukhi Poribar Call Center: 10626

Customers Right Helpline: 16400

Public Basic liberties Commission Helpline: 16209

Public Helpline for Government Lawful Guide Administrations: 1025

Land Helpline: 1055

NID Helpline: 16204

Birth Enrollment Helpline: 1055

Bangladesh Bank Hotline: 16229
Service of Ostracizes' Government assistance and Abroad Work: 16206
Farming Call Community: 16123
Krisho Bondhu-Krishi Batayon: 16123
BTRC Helpline: 16232
BTCL Call focus: 16207
UP Helpline (ইউনিয়ন পরিষদ (হেল্পলাইন): 109
DESCO Hotline: 16231
DPDC Hotline: 16231
NESCO Hotline: 16231
WZPDCL hotline: 16231
E-GP Hotline: 16231
Dhaka WASA Helpline: 16205

Chapter 10. Sustainable Travel

Bangladesh is a delightful and different country with a rich social legacy. Likewise a nation is confronting various ecological difficulties. Accordingly, the travel industry is turning out to be progressively significant in Bangladesh.

Reasonable the travel industry is tied in with limiting the effect of the travel industry on the climate and nearby networks. It is tied in with tracking down ways of voyaging that are both charming and dependable.

There are various ways of rehearsing reasonable travel in Bangladesh. The following are a couple of tips:

Remain in eco-accommodating facilities. There are a developing number of eco-accommodating lodgings and guesthouses in Bangladesh. These facilities utilise sustainable power sources, limit waste, and backing nearby networks.

Eco Friendly convenience in Bangladesh

Take public transportation. Bangladesh has a decent open transportation framework, including transports, trains, and ships. Taking public transportation is an incredible method for diminishing your carbon impression and setting aside cash.

Public transportation in Bangladesh

Eat neighbourhood food. Eating neighbourhood food is an extraordinary method for supporting the nearby economy and lessening your ecological effect. Bangladesh has a heavenly and various food, so make certain to attempt a portion of the neighbourhood dishes while you are there.

Neighbourhood food in Bangladesh

Regard the neighbourhood culture. Bangladesh is a Muslim-greater part country, so it is essential to be conscious of the nearby culture and customs. This incorporates dressing unassumingly and staying away from public showcases of friendship.

Individuals in Bangladesh dressed humbly

Support neighbourhood organisations. While purchasing keepsakes or different products, attempt to help neighbourhood organisations. This will assist with supporting the neighbourhood economy and make occupations.

Nearby organisations in Bangladesh

The following are a couple of explicit instances of economical the travel industry exercises in Bangladesh:

Visit the Sundarbans. The Sundarbans is the biggest mangrove woods on the planet and it is home to an assortment of untamed life, including the Bengal tiger. There are various visit administrators that offer feasible voyages through the Sundarbans.

Sundarbans in Bangladesh

Visit the Chittagong Slope Lots. The Chittagong Slope Plots is a rocky locale in southeastern Bangladesh. It is home to various native people groups who have their own novel societies and customs. There are various visit administrators that offer manageable voyages through the Chittagong Slope Plots.

Chittagong Slope Lots in Bangladesh

Visit the Regal Bengal Safari Park. The Regal Bengal Safari Park is a natural life park that is home to different creatures, including the Bengal tiger. The recreation area is focused economically on the travel industry and it has various drives set up to safeguard the climate.

Responsible Tourism

The travel industry in Bangladesh is a sort of the travel industry that means to limit the adverse consequences of the travel industry on the climate, culture, and society of the country. A kind of the travel industry is practical and helpful for both the vacationers and the nearby local area.

There are various ways of rehearsing capable the travel industry in Bangladesh, including:

Supporting nearby organisations: While picking convenience, eateries, and visit administrators, attempt to pick those that are possessed and worked by local people. This will assist with guaranteeing that the advantages of the travel industry are straightforwardly imparted to the neighbourhood local area.

Regarding neighbourhood culture and customs: Bangladesh is a Muslim-greater part country, so it is vital to be conscious of nearby traditions and dress unassumingly while visiting strict destinations. It is likewise critical to know about the country's severe medication regulations.

Moderating normal assets: Bangladesh is a country with a rich regular legacy, so it is essential to be aware of your effect on the climate. This implies lessening your waste, rationing water, and abstaining from littering.

Safeguarding natural life: Bangladesh is home to an assortment of one of a kind natural life animal categories, so it is vital to be deferential to their environments. This implies abstaining from taking care of or hassling creatures, and not taking keepsakes from public parks and other safeguarded regions.

Here are a few explicit instances of mindful the travel industry in Bangladesh:

Visiting a nearby town: There are various visit administrators that deal voyages through nearby towns in Bangladesh. This is an incredible method for finding out about the nearby culture and lifestyle, and to help the neighbourhood local area.

Going on a boat outing through the Sundarbans: The Sundarbans is an UNESCO World Legacy Site that is home to an assortment of remarkable untamed life, including the Bengal tiger. There are various visit administrators that propose boat trips through the Sundarbans, which is an incredible method for seeing the natural life and finding out about the environment.

Chipping in at a nearby task: There are various worker associations in Bangladesh that work on different ventures, like schooling, medical care, and ecological protection. Chipping in is an extraordinary method for rewarding the neighbourhood local area and to more deeply study the country.

Eco-Friendly Practices

Mindful the travel industry in Bangladesh is a kind of the travel industry that expects to limit the adverse consequence of the travel industry on the climate, culture, and society of the country. A sort of the travel industry is reasonable and valuable for both the sightseers and the nearby local area.

There are various ways of rehearsing mindful the travel industry in Bangladesh, including:

Supporting neighbourhood organisations: While picking convenience, cafés, and visit administrators, attempt to pick those that are claimed and worked by local people. This will assist with guaranteeing that the advantages of the travel industry are straightforwardly imparted to the nearby local area.

Regarding neighbourhood culture and customs: Bangladesh is a Muslim-greater part country, so it is critical to be conscious of nearby traditions and dress unassumingly while visiting strict destinations. It is likewise essential to know about the country's severe medication regulations.

Moderating regular assets: Bangladesh is a country with a rich normal legacy, so it is vital to be aware of your effect on the climate. This implies decreasing your waste, moderating water, and abstaining from littering.

Safeguarding natural life: Bangladesh is home to an assortment of exceptional natural life species, so it is critical to be deferential to their environments. This implies abstaining from taking care of or badgering creatures, and not taking trinkets from public parks and other safeguarded regions.

Here are a few explicit instances of mindful the travel industry in Bangladesh:

Visiting a nearby town: There are various visit administrators that proposition voyages through nearby towns in Bangladesh. This is an extraordinary method for finding out about the nearby culture and lifestyle, and to help the neighbourhood local area.

Going on a boat outing through the Sundarbans: The Sundarbans is an UNESCO World Legacy Site that is home to an assortment of extraordinary untamed life, including the Bengal tiger. There are various visit administrators that deal boat trips through the Sundarbans, which is an incredible method for seeing the natural life and finding out about the biological system.

Chipping in at a neighbourhood project: There are various worker associations in Bangladesh that work on different activities, like training, medical services, and ecological preservation. Chipping in is an extraordinary method for rewarding the nearby local area and to get more familiar with the country

Bangladesh is a thickly populated country with a quickly creating economy. This has prompted various natural difficulties, like air and water contamination, deforestation, and waste administration issues. Nonetheless, there is a developing consciousness of the significance of natural security in Bangladesh, and various eco-accommodating practices are being taken on by people, networks, and organisations.

Here are a few instances of eco-accommodating practices in Bangladesh:

Practical agribusiness: Ranchers are progressively embracing feasible agrarian practices, like harvest revolution, treating the soil, and incorporating bug the board. These practices help to diminish the utilisation of compound composts and pesticides, which can contaminate the climate.

Sustainable power: Bangladesh is putting resources into environmentally friendly power sources, for example, sun oriented and wind power. This is assisting with diminishing the country's dependence on petroleum products and decreasing ozone depleting substance discharges.

Squander the board: Bangladesh is further developing its waste administration framework. This incorporates fabricating new landfills and incinerators, and advancing reusing and fertilising the soil.

Backwoods protection: Bangladesh is attempting to preserve its backwoods, which assume a significant part in safeguarding the climate and giving occupations to rustic networks.

Eco-tourism: Bangladesh is advancing the eco-the travel industry, which is a kind of the travel industry that means to limit the adverse consequences of the travel industry on the climate. This incorporates empowering vacationers to visit safeguarded regions and to help neighbourhood organisations.

Notwithstanding these particular practices, there are various different things that Bangladeshis are doing to live more eco-accommodating ways of life. For instance, more individuals are utilising energy-proficient apparatuses, reusing their waste, and strolling or cycling as opposed to driving.

These eco-accommodating practices are assisting with making Bangladesh a more reasonable country. Notwithstanding, there is even more work to be finished. The public authority, organisations, and people all need to cooperate to safeguard the climate and make a manageable future for Bangladesh.

Supporting Local Communities

There are numerous ways of supporting nearby networks in Bangladesh. The following are a couple of thoughts:

Support nearby organisations and associations. At the point when you purchase labour and products from neighbourhood organisations, you are assisting with supporting the nearby economy and making occupations. You can likewise uphold nearby associations by giving your time or cash.

Volunteer your time. There are numerous associations in Bangladesh that depend on volunteers to assist them with conveying fundamental administrations. You can chip in your opportunity to show English, assist with calamity help, or work on local area advancement projects.

Give to noble causes that help Bangladesh. There are numerous foundations that work to work on the existence of individuals in Bangladesh. You can give to noble causes that help instruction, medical services, debacle alleviation, or different causes that you care about.

Advocate for arrangements that help Bangladesh. You can advocate for strategies that help Bangladesh by reaching your chosen authorities and telling them that you care about the country. You can likewise uphold associations that are attempting to advance strategies that will help Bangladesh.

Here are a few explicit instances of how you can uphold nearby networks in Bangladesh:

Support nearby ranchers. Bangladesh is a rural nation, and many individuals depend on cultivating for their vocation. You can uphold nearby ranchers by purchasing their produce straightforwardly from them or from neighbourhood ranchers markets. You can likewise uphold associations that are attempting to work on agrarian practices and efficiency in Bangladesh.

Support schooling. Schooling is fundamental for individuals to lift themselves out of neediness and work on their lives. You can uphold training in Bangladesh by giving to schools or supporting a kid's schooling. You can likewise chip in your opportunity to show English or different subjects.

Support medical services. Medical services are quite difficult for some individuals in Bangladesh. You can uphold medical services in Bangladesh by giving to emergency clinics or centres. You can likewise chip in your opportunity to furnish clinical consideration or to assist with general wellbeing drives.

Support debacle alleviation. Bangladesh is inclined to catastrophic events, like floods, twisters, and dry spells. You can uphold catastrophe help in Bangladesh by giving to associations that are attempting to give help to casualties of debacles. You can likewise chip in your opportunity to assist with calamity aid projects.

Chapter 11 Resources and further information

Bangladesh is a country with a rich history and culture, and there are numerous assets accessible to more deeply study it. The following are a couple of ideas:

Legislature of Bangladesh site: This site contains an abundance of data about the nation, including its set of experiences, government, economy, and culture. You can likewise track down data on the travel industry, schooling, and business.

Banglapedia: Banglapedia is a public reference book of Bangladesh. It is an extensive and legitimate wellspring of data on all parts of the country.

Bangladesh Public Gallery: The Bangladesh Public Historical centre is the biggest gallery in the nation and houses an assortment of relics and shows that recount the tale of Bangladesh's set of experiences and culture.

The Freedom War Gallery: The Freedom War Historical centre is devoted to the Bangladesh Freedom Battle of 1971. It houses an assortment of curios, photos, and records that recount the narrative of the conflict and the penances that were made.

Dhaka College: Dhaka College is the most established and most lofty college in Bangladesh. It has a library with a huge assortment of books and articles on Bangladesh and different themes.

Notwithstanding these assets, there are numerous different books, sites, and narratives that give data about Bangladesh. The following are a couple of ideas:

Books:

Bangladesh: A Set of experiences by Willem van Schendel

The Collection of memoirs of Sheik Mujibur Rahman

The Eager Tide by Amitav Ghosh

Stream of Smoke by Amitav Ghosh

Sites:

The Everyday Star (English-language paper)

Prothom Alo (Bangla-language paper)

The Bangladesh Spectator (English-language government paper)

Narratives:

The Unconquerable (2007)

Offspring of the Fog (2013)

Made in Bangladesh (2015)

Useful Websites and Apps

Here are a few valuable sites and applications in Bangladesh:

Sites

Administration of Bangladesh: This is the authority site of the Public authority of Bangladesh, where you can find data on all taxpayer supported organisations, strategies, and drives.

Banglapedia: This is the Public Reference book of Bangladesh, where you can track down data on all parts of Bangladeshi culture, history, and society.

Bangladesh Bank: This is the national bank of Bangladesh, where you can track down data on the nation's economy, monetary framework, and money related approaches.

Bangladesh Protections and Trade Commission: This is the administrative body for the Bangladesh financial exchange, where you can find data on上市公司、交易、投资和市场数据。

Bangladesh Leading body of Schooling: This is the overseeing body for schooling in Bangladesh, where you can track down data on the educational plan, assessments, and instructive foundations.

Applications

bKash: This is the most famous portable banking application in Bangladesh, which permits clients to send and get cash, take care of bills, and re-energize their cell phones.

Rocket: This is another famous versatile banking application in Bangladesh, which offers comparable administrations to bKash.

Shohoz: This is a super application that offers various administrations, including ride-hailing, food conveyance, and web based shopping.

Pathao: This is one more super application that offers comparative administrations to Shohoz.

Chaldal: This is an internet based staple conveyance application that permits clients to arrange food from their number one stores and have them conveyed to their entryway.

Foodpanda: This is an internet based food conveyance application that permits clients to arrange food from their number one eateries and have it conveyed to their entryway.

Bikroy: Here clients can trade different labour and products.

Recommended Reading

Bangladesh has a rich scholarly practice, going back hundreds of years. Probably the most observed Bengali essayists, like Rabindranath Tagore, Kazi Nazrul Islam, and Bankim Chandra Chatterjee, were brought into the world in Bangladesh. Lately, another age of Bangladeshi scholars has arisen, earning global respect for their work.

Here is a rundown of suggested perusing in Bangladesh, including both work of art and contemporary works:

Ekattorer Dinguli (Long periods of '71) by Jahanara Imam: This diary is a strong record of the Bangladesh Freedom Battle, as seen by a young lady living in Dhaka.

A Brilliant Age by Tahmima Anam: This clever recounts the tale of a family living in Dhaka during the Bangladesh Freedom War.

Pather Panchali (Tune of the Street) by Bibhutibhushan Bandopadhyay: This novel is an exemplary story about growing up set in rustic Bengal.

Chosen Brief tales by Rabindranath Tagore: Tagore was a productive essayist, and his brief tales are a portion of his best work.

Those Days by Sunil Gangopadhyay: This novel is a moving story of adoration and misfortune, set in Kolkata during the Parcel of India.

Lajja (Disgrace) by Taslima Nasrin: This novel is a strong incrimination of strict narrow mindedness and viciousness.

Block Path by Monica Ali: This original recounts the tale of a youthful Bangladeshi lady who weds an English man and moves to London.

The Great Muslim by Tahmima Anam: This clever recounts the narrative of a youthful Bangladeshi man who is attempting to accommodate his confidence with his cutting edge way of life.

The Bones of Beauty by Tahmima Anam: This original recounts the tale of a youthful Bangladeshi lady who is looking for her character in the aftermath of the Bangladesh Freedom War.

Samira Surfs by Rukhsana Khan: This centre grade novel recounts the tale of a youthful Rohingya exile young lady who finds strength and sisterhood in a nearby surf club for young ladies.

Hani and Ishu's Manual for Counterfeit Dating by Adiba Jaigirdar: This youthful grown-up clever recounts the narrative of two Bangladeshi-American young people who phoney dating each other to prevail upon their pounds.

Abandon the World by Rumaan Alam: This clever recounts the tale of two families who are put together during a baffling emergency. One of the families is Bangladeshi-American.

Language and Travel Phrases

Language
The official language of Bangladesh is Bengali. It is spoken by more than 98% of the populace. English is likewise generally spoken, particularly in metropolitan regions and in the public authority and business areas.

Here are a few essential Bengali expressions that might be valuable for voyagers:

Hello: Namaskar (formal), Salam (casual)

Farewell: Farewell (formal), Alvida (casual)

If it's not too much trouble: Doya kore (formal), Kichu shomoy (casual)

Much obliged to you: Dhonyobad (formal), Dhonno (casual)

Indeed: Haa

No: Na

Do you communicate in English?: Aapni ki ingreji bolte paren?

I don't communicate in Bengali: Ami bangla bolte pari na.

Travel Expressions

Here are some valuable travel phrases in Bengali:

How much is this?: Estimated time of arrival koto taka?

Where could the washroom be?: Shauchalaya ?

Could you at any point help me?: Aapni ki amar shohayta korte paren?

I really want a taxi: Amar ekta taxi lagbe.

Where might I at any point track down lodging?: Ami inn pabo?

I'm lost: Ami rasta haraye felsechi.

I really want a specialist: Amar ekta specialist lagbe.

I want the police: Amar police.

Tips

Bengalis are for the most part amicable and inviting individuals. Don't hesitate for even a moment to take a stab at talking a couple of Bengali expressions of Bengali, regardless of whether you commit errors.

Assuming that you're experiencing difficulty imparting, take a stab at utilising signals or pointing at things.

A great many people in metropolitan regions will speak some English, however it's consistently really smart to gain proficiency with a couple of essential Bengali expressions, particularly in the event that you're wanting to make a trip to country regions.

Be aware of Bangladeshi culture and customs. For instance, dress unassumingly and keep away from public presentations of warmth.

Chapter 12. Appendices

Supplements in Bangladesh are regularly used to give extra data that isn't crucial for the fundamental body of a report. They might contain such things as:

Definite information tables

Specialised determinations

Supporting documentation

Glossary of terms

References

Book index

File

Reference sections are normally positioned toward the finish of a report, after the body text and any notes or endnotes. They are numbered consecutively, and every informative supplement ought to be given an illustrative title.

Here are a few instances of how supplements are utilised in Bangladesh:

An administration report on the economy could incorporate a supplement with itemised information tables on Gross domestic product development, expansion, and other monetary markers.

An examination paper on another clinical treatment could incorporate a reference section with specialised details for the treatment and supporting documentation from clinical preliminaries.

A strategic plan could incorporate a supplement with a glossary of terms and references.

A book on a perplexing subject could incorporate a reference section with a list of sources and record.

Supplements can be an important instrument for furnishing perusers with extra data that they might see as supportive. Notwithstanding, it is vital to utilise them reasonably, and to guarantee that the data they contain is important and essential.

Here are a few ways to compose successful reference sections:

Ensure that the data in the supplement is pertinent to the fundamental body of the report.

Coordinate the data in a reasonable and coherent manner.

Use headings and subheadings to make the data simple to check.

Use tables and figures to introduce information in a reasonable and succinct manner.

Characterise any specialised terms or abbreviations. Edit the informative supplement cautiously prior to submitting it.

How to get maps of key Regions

The most effective method to get guides of key districts in Bangladesh:

There are various ways of getting guides of key districts in Bangladesh, including:

Online guides: There are various web-based map benefits that give itemised guides of Bangladesh, including Google Guides, Bing Guides, and OpenStreetMaps. These administrations permit you to see maps at various zoom levels and to see various kinds of elements, like streets, streams, and structures.

Government sites: The Bangladesh government likewise gives various guides of the nation, including guides of authoritative divisions, locale, and upazilas. These guides can be downloaded from the sites of the Bangladesh Agency of Insights and the Bangladesh Public Geospatial Data Framework.

Privately owned businesses: There are likewise various privately owned businesses that sell guides of Bangladesh. These guides can be found at book shops and online retailers.

Instances of key districts in Bangladesh:

Dhaka: The capital of Bangladesh and the most crowded city in the country.

Chattogram: The second biggest city in Bangladesh and a significant port city.

Sylhet: A city in northeastern Bangladesh known for its tea manors and regular magnificence.

Cox's Bazar: A waterfront town in southeastern Bangladesh known for its long sandy ocean side.

Cox's Bazar, Bangladesh map

The most effective method to involve guides of key districts in Bangladesh:

Guides of key districts in Bangladesh can be utilised for different purposes, for example,

Navigation: Guides can be utilised to explore around Bangladesh, whether you are driving, strolling, or taking public transportation.

Planning: Guides can be utilised to design trips and to distinguish key spots to visit.

Research: Guides can be utilised for research purposes, like concentrating on the nation's topography, socioeconomics, and economy.

Ways to involve guides of key districts in Bangladesh:

Utilise different sources: There are various guides of Bangladesh accessible, so it means a lot to utilise different sources to get the most reliable and state-of-the-art data.

Know about the scale: Guides can be drawn at various scales, so it is critical to know about the size of the guide you are utilising. This will assist you with understanding the degree of detail that is remembered for the guide.

Utilise the legend: The legend is a key that makes sense of the images and tones utilised on the guide. Counselling the legend prior to utilising the map is significant.

Arrange yourself: Prior to utilising a guide, it is useful to situate yourself by recognizing a few important milestones, like waterways, streets, and urban communities. This will assist you with getting your direction and to grasp the format of the guide.

Sample itineraries

Bangladesh is a wonderful and different country with a rich culture and history. There are various spots to visit and what should be done in Bangladesh, contingent upon your inclinations.

Here are some example agendas for various sorts of voyagers:

7-day schedule for nature darlings:

Show up in Dhaka and look into your lodging. Visit the Lalbagh Stronghold, a seventeenth century Mughal post complex.

Fly to Sylhet, a city in the upper east of Bangladesh known for its tea manors and lavish green slopes. Visit the Lawachara Public Park, home to an assortment of untamed life, including the endangered hoolock gibbon.

Require a roadtrip to the Srimangal Tea Domain, one of the biggest tea bequests in Bangladesh. Find out about the tea-production process and partake in some newly fermented tea.

 Fly back to Dhaka.

Go on a boat outing to the Sundarbans, an UNESCO World Legacy Site and the biggest mangrove backwoods on the planet. Go on a natural life safari to detect tigers, crocodiles, monkeys, and different creatures.

Get back to Dhaka.

Leave from Dhaka.

7-day schedule for history and culture buffs:

Show up in Dhaka and look into your inn. Visit the Public Exhibition hall of Bangladesh, which houses an assortment of relics from the country's rich history.

Visit the Ahsan Manzil, a nineteenth century castle that was once the home of the Nawab of Dhaka. Visit the close by Star Mosque, a wonderful mosque with star-moulded themes on its roof.

Require a roadtrip to Bagerhat, a city in the south of Bangladesh that is home to the remnants of a middle age Muslim city. Visit the Sixty Vault Mosque, an UNESCO World Legacy Site, and the Burial chamber of Khan Jahan Ali, the organiser behind Bagerhat.

Fly to Chittagong, the second-biggest city in Bangladesh. Visit the Ethnological Exhibition hall, which houses an assortment of relics from the different ethnic gatherings of Bangladesh.

Visit the Pahartali Buddhist Sanctuary, the biggest Buddhist sanctuary in Chittagong.

Fly back to Dhaka.

Withdraw from Dhaka.

7-day agenda for ocean side darlings:

Show up in Cox's Bazar, home to the world's longest solid oceanside. Look into your inn and loosen up around the ocean.

Go on a boat outing to Sonadia Island, a wonderful island found simply off the shoreline of Cox's Bazar. Appreciate swimming, swimming, and sunbathing on the island.

Visit the Himchari Cascade, a lovely cascade situated in the slopes behind Cox's Bazar.

Fly to Dhaka.

Visit the Greenhouse, an enormous park with different plants and blossoms.

Visit the Dhakeshwari Sanctuary, the biggest Hindu sanctuary in Bangladesh.

Leave from Dhaka.

These are only a couple of test schedules for Bangladesh. You can tweak your agenda to accommodate your inclinations and financial plan.

Packing Checklist

Pressing Agenda for Bangladesh

Clothing

Unobtrusive dress that covers your shoulders and knees is suggested, particularly in additional moderate regions.

Baggy, normal textures like cotton and cloth are great for the warm and muggy climate.

Pack a light coat or sweater for cooler nights and cooled spaces.

Agreeable shoes, like shoes or shoes, are an unquestionable requirement.

A cap, shades, and sunscreen are fundamental for safeguarding yourself from the sun.

Toiletries and Drugs

Bring your typical toiletries, like cleanser, conditioner, cleanser, toothpaste, and antiperspirant.

Bug repellent is fundamental for shielding yourself from mosquitoes and different bugs.

Assuming you are taking any doctor prescribed meds, make certain to pack enough for your whole outing.

It is likewise really smart to pack an essential emergency treatment unit, including things like swathes, pain killers, and germ-free wipes.

Different Basics

Identification, visa, and other travel archives

Cash and Visas

Telephone charger

Camera

Connector (if vital)

Whatever other things that you really want or need on your outing, like books, music, or games

Extra Tips

It is smart to pack light, particularly on the off chance that you are anticipating doing a ton of going around Bangladesh.

Dress in layers so you can conform to the evolving temperature.

Bring a reusable water container to remain hydrated.

Make certain to pack any social attire that you might require for unique events.

Regard nearby traditions and customs.

What not to pack

Uncovering clothing

Liquor (which is unlawful in Bangladesh)

Pork items (which are likewise unlawful in Bangladesh)

Strict materials that might be viewed as hostile

A lot of money

Pressing for explicit exercises

In the event that you are anticipating doing a particular exercise in Bangladesh, for example, journeying or visiting the Sundarbans, make certain to pack the suitable dress and stuff. For instance, in the event that you will be journeying, you will require solid shoes, a happy dress, and a cap. In the event that you are visiting the Sundarbans, you will require bug repellent, sunscreen, and a cap.

Made in United States
Troutdale, OR
12/21/2023

16274648R00076